Songs of the Kingdom

Third Edition

Acknowledgments

Project Manager
Geoff Fawcett

Senior Music Editor
Sherwin Mackintosh

Musical Editors
Stephen Arthur Allen, Patrick Kapterian, Donald Vega, Paul May, Joe Farmer, J. Brian Craig

Cover Design
Jennifer Maugel, Chris Costello, Toney Mulhollan

Interior Layout and Copy
Micro Music: Reid Lancaster
Con Brio Music Typesetting: Evan Conlee
Additional Layout: Toney Mulhollan

Songs of the Kingdom—Third Edition
© 2015 by Disciples Today, Inc.

All rights reserved.
No part of this book may be duplicated, copied, translated, reproduced or stored mechanically or electronically without specific, written permission of Disciples Today, Inc.

Distributed in association with Illumination Publishers, 6010 Pinecreek Ridge Court, Spring, Texas 77379, USA.

ISBN: 978-1-941988-01-5

To order additional copies of *Songs of the Kingdom* songbook go to www.ipibooks.com.

A Spiritual Singing Lesson

E. Sherwin Mackintosh
Senior Music Editor

Since the beginning of time, God has surrounded himself with singing. He taught the morning stars to sing at creation (Job 38:7) and leads the thousands of angels who constantly sing around his throne. Yet nothing pleases him more than the singing of individuals whose hearts are tuned to him.

Throughout my Christian life, people have often asked me, "Can you teach me how to sing?" and "How do you learn how to sing?" Here is a spiritual singing lesson—not a lesson in singing the right notes or understanding four-part harmony, but a lesson on what the Bible teaches about our singing.

I Can Sing

A lot of people come into the kingdom of God either seeing themselves as a singer or a nonsinger, either as having the talent or not. While I believe that some people are more naturally gifted than others, the Scriptures make it abundantly clear that we are all to be singers. Psalm 96:1 says to "sing to the Lord, all the earth." It says "all the earth," not just a few select individuals. Paul exhorts us to "sing and make music in your heart to the Lord" (Ephesians 5:19). He does not say to sing if that is your gift or if you have studied music. It is a command for all Christians. It may be something that we have to learn how to do, just like we have to learn to study the Bible or share our faith. It may take some time, it may take some work, it may even take a little money, but it's something we all have to work on. Even the most talented singers who become Christians have to learn how God wants them to sing. What used to be a performance medium for them must now become part of a relationship. But God has promised all of us that we "can do everything through him who gives [us] strength" (Philippians 4:13). This includes singing!

Spirit and the Mind

God does give us specific instructions on how to sing. Paul says, "I will pray with the spirit, but I will also pray with my mind. I will sing with my spirit, but I will also sing with my mind" (1 Corinthians 14:15). In our movement we need to maintain the important balance between the youthfulness of the "Spirit" with the maturity of the "mind."

When we sing a song like "O Lord, Prepare Me," we love the feel of the song, and we are moved by the spirit of the music, but often we do not realize the meaning of what we are singing. In this song we are praying directly to God and saying, in essence, "Give me your hardest trial, your toughest situation, because I want to be pure and holy, tried and true; I want to be a living sanctuary for you." The song contrasts the concept of the sanctuary in the Old Testament with that of the New Testament. The sanctuary of the Old Law was a physical building where God's spirit actually lived. Today, thanks to Jesus Christ, our bodies are to be the living temple of God. We are pledging our own bodies to be a holy temple in which God can live. These deeper concepts require more than just a casual reading of the text, but the discipline to focus on what they mean.

On the other hand, sometimes we know what the words mean. Our minds are in gear, but the Spirit is lacking. We sing a song like "Joyful, Joyful, We Adore Thee," and the last thing we see on our faces is joy! The conviction and power needed to preach the song are missing.

The biggest danger is when we become very comfortable with a song and sing without the Spirit or our mind. We mindlessly repeat phrases that mean nothing to us. We honor him with our lips, but our hearts are far from him (Mark 7:6). These words need to mean something to us personally, or we should not be singing them. We must sing with the Spirit and our minds.

Communication

Our singing is always communication. We are either singing to God, Jesus, the Holy Spirit, our brothers and sisters or to people who are not yet Christians. Ephesians 5:19 says to "speak to one another" in our singing. When we come to a worship service, we are literally taking refuge from a battle. Satan has been waging a war for our souls all week, and we are pulling together to encourage each other. When we sing "Don't You Want to Go to That Land," we are taking each other's spiritual pulse. We are asking, "Are you still with us?" and "Don't you want to go with us?" and "I'm on my way; I'm bound!" We are speaking to one another in our singing. When we sing "Rise up, O Men of God," we are calling each other to arms: "We need your help! Rise up and make the church great." We are spurring one another on (Hebrews 10:24), preparing each other to go back into battle.

We need to think more about speaking the songs than singing them. Somehow when we add a melody to words, what used to be a prayer is now "just a song." The music is mainly a vehicle to express the text. Each song that we sing is important and is not to be taken lightly. When Moses was teaching the Israelites a song, he told the people that the song was "not just idle words;...they are your life" (Deuteronomy 32:47). We need to communicate each word of every song.

Psalms, Hymns and Spiritual Songs

In both Ephesians and Philippians, God speaks through Paul, saying that we are to sing "psalms, hymns and spiritual songs." This may, at first, look like three words for the same thing, but Paul is indicating three distinct forms of songs: "psalms" are taken directly from Scripture; "hymns" are based on Scripture and expound on the deeper insights of the subject; and "spiritual songs" are those that come from our hearts, our emotions. We need to love all three types of songs, not just the kinds that appeal to us musically.

For many of us our taste in music is very personal. Some of us might like classical music and hate heavy metal, while others might think that rap music is the only true form of musical expression. Paul isn't offering this as a musical choice. He is telling us to sing all three types—psalms, hymns and spiritual songs—because each type ministers to a certain area of our hearts. They are essential to our spiritual health. While the emotional quality of the spiritual songs may appeal to some of us on a surface level, we also need the depth found in a hymn. On the other hand, those of us who are very comfortable with the hymns need the spontaneity and outward focus that a spiritual song can give. We all need the psalms to help us learn and memorize Scripture. We need a balance of all three.

A New Song

Psalm 40:3 says that "He [God] put a new song in my mouth." I believe that God has given every Christian a unique song to sing, literally, a new song to sing. It might be personal, sung only to God, or it might be a song that thousands of disciples will sing around the world. Its purpose might be to deepen another person's faith or to cause thousands more to become Christians. God is the author of creativity and has placed many songs in our hearts that are waiting to be written down. In Deuteronomy 32, God gave Moses a new song. He told Moses to "write it down." Moses did so that very day. God used Moses as an instrument to write it down and to teach the Israelites. He said that the song would serve as a witness for him. Long after they had forgotten everything that Moses had taught them and had actually turned away from God, this song would remind them of what God had done for them. As disciples, I believe that we often have songs that God gives to us, and we do not do anything with them. Sometimes I think that God tries to speak through us, but we do not take time to stop and listen to the song God has for us. The challenge is for us to listen and "write it down."

We need to take this spiritual singing lesson seriously. Jesus sang with his disciples (Matthew 26:30) and wants us to sing with him as his modern-day disciples. God wants us to restore Biblical singing in our own relationship with him. Then, when anyone walks into our fellowship and hears the beauty and conviction of our singing, they cannot help but fall down on their knees and proclaim, "God is really among you!" (1 Corinthians 14:25).

General Index

Section	Starting Number
Psalms	1
Hymns	200
Christmas Carols	550
Spiritual Songs	600
Special Arrangements	800
Devotional & Children's Songs	900

(Italic text denotes first line.)

A Faithful Witness 222
A Mighty Fortress 360
A Stream in the Desert 215
Abba Father 221
Abide with Me 478
Ain't No Rock 900
Alas! And Did My Savior Bleed? 431
All Hail the Power (Traditional) 476
All Hail the Power 881
All to Jesus I Surrender 474
Always Triumphant 211
Amazing Grace (Traditional) 359
Amazing Grace 800
Amen 701
Anchor For the Soul 223
Angels We Have Heard on High 554
Are you standing in the place that will stand forever? ... 605
Arise, My Soul, Arise 473
As For Me and My House 224
As Many As Possible 801
Awesome God 445
Be Still and Know I Am God 2
Be Still, My Soul 465
Be Strong, Take Heart 220
Be with Me, Lord 209
Beneath the Cross of Jesus 454
Blessed Assurance 451
Blue skies and rainbows 933
Breathe on Me, Breath of God 468
Building Up the Kingdom 932
By Faith 225
Captives came back into Zion 204
Christ, the Lord, Is Risen Today 452
Christ, We Do All Adore Thee 475
Come, we that love the Lord 459
Come and go with me to my Father's house ... 911
Cornerstone 226
Create in Me a Pure Heart (for men) ... 804
Create in Me a Pure Heart (SATB) 1
Crossing Over 702
Crown Him with Many Crowns 437
Deep Down in My Heart 903
Deeper 230
Don't You Wanna Go? 705
E-Khaya (Hallelujah!) 703
Eloi 227

Encamped along the hills of light 434
Encourage My Soul 704
Entrusted 228
Even Greater Things 229
Fairest Lord Jesus 453
Faith Is the Victory 434
Father God, whom we seek first 210
Father, if not for your mercy 600
Feed My Sheep 232
Fill My Soul 233
Finish the Race 231
Follow Me 439
For All Generations 234
For the Beauty of the Earth 470
For Those Tears, I Died 362
Give Me Oil in My Lamp 904
Give thanks to the Lord, for he is good ... 4
Glorious Things of Thee Are Spoken ... 352
Glory Be to Jesus 366
Glory, Glory (Laid My Burdens Down) ... 711
Glory, Glory, Hallelujah (Traditional) ... 458
Glory, Glory, Hallelujah 802
Go and Make Disciples 214
God Almighty Reigns 216
God Alone 803
God Alone is Good 115
God Is So Good 706
God Moves in a Mysterious Way 361
God of Our Fathers 368
God Will Do Everything 236
Great Among the Nations 206
Great Is Thy Faithfulness 436
Greater Worth Than Gold 237
Ha-La-La-La-Le-Lu-Jah 902
Hallelujah 202
Hallelujah Chorus 880
Hallelujah! Praise Jehovah! 433
Hallelujah! What a Savior! 450
Hard Fighting Soldier 708
Hark! The Herald Angels Sing 557
Have Thine Own Way 432
Have You Not Heard? 3
He Gave Her Water 707
He Is Lord! 709
He Must Become Greater 235
He said to go to ev'ry nation 214
He's On Time 606
Heavenly Sunlight 428
Here Am I Send Me 238
Higher Ground 240
His Banner over Me Is Love 905
His Eye Is on the Sparrow 713
His Hands 241
His Love Endures Forever 4
Hold to God's Unchanging Hand 367
Holy Father 395
Holy, Holy, Holy 442
Holy is the Lord 242
Holy Perfect Always Forever 243

Home in Heaven	607
Home With You	239
How Firm a Foundation	443
How Great Thou Art	387
How Majestic Is Your Name	113
How Sweet, How Heavenly	370
Humble Yourself in the Sight of the Lord	104
I Am a Poor, Wayfaring Stranger	710
I Am Not Afraid	112
I Am Resolved	372
I am weak, but thou art strong	472
I Can't Keep It to Myself	712
I Feel Good	714
I Have Decided to Follow Jesus	716
I Hear God Singing to Me	217
I heard an old, old story	357
I know not why God's wondrous grace	425
I Know That My Redeemer Lives	462
I Know That My Redeemer Lives (Messiah)	376
I Know Whom I Have Believed	425
I Love to Praise His Holy Name	722
I Love to Tell the Story	418
I Love Your Word	246
I may never march in the infantry	931
I Need Thee Every Hour	430
I Need Your Love	218
I once was lost in sin	448
I pray, O Lord Jesus, my love you'd increase	200
I said I wasn't gonna talk about it	712
I The Created	245
I traveled down a lonely road	439
I Tried and I Tried	737, 906
I Walk with the King	426
I Want Jesus to Walk with Me	715
I Want to Be Less	244
I want to be like Jesus	903
I was lost; now I'm found	212
I was sinking deep in sin	414
I Will Call upon the Lord	103
I will laugh and sing my anthems	216
I Will Sing the Wondrous Story	449
I Will Speak	466
If life is just a song, I will sing for you	203
If You Want to Love Him	610
I'll Be a Friend to Jesus	420
I'll Be Listening	717
I'll Fly Away	422
I'm Building Me A Home	608
I'm Coming Up, Lord	718
I'm Going to Praise You	609
I'm Gonna View That Holy City	909
I'm Happy Today	907
I'm in the Lord's Army	931
I'm in the way, the bright and shining way	399
I'm Not Ashamed to Own My Lord	460
I'm thirsty and hungry and longing	215
Immortal, Invisible, God Only Wise	407
In My Father's House	911
In the Kingdom	605
In the morning when you rise	602
Isaiah saw that it would come	206
It Came upon a Midnight Clear	553
It Is Well with My Soul	456
It's me (it's me), it's me, O Lord	923
I've Been Redeemed	725
I've got peace like a river	920
I've Got the Joy, Joy, Joy	912
Jesus Is Lord (Trad.)	423
Jesus Is Lord	805
Jesus Is Well and Alive Today	933
Jesus, Keep Me near the Cross	419
Jesus Loves Me!	424
Jesus Loves the Little Children	910
Jesus Will Fix It	719
Jordan River	729
Joy to the World	552
Joyful, Joyful, We Adore Thee	464
Just a Closer Walk with Thee	472
Just a Little Talk with Jesus	448
Just As I Am	471
King of my life, I crown thee now	429
King of the Jungle	930
Kyrie Eleison (Lord, Have Mercy)	201
Lamb of God	417
Lead Me to Calvary	429
Lead Me to Some Soul Today	421
Lead Me to the Rock	119
Let Us Break Bread Together	721
Let the Light Shine Down	255
Let the Peoples Praise You	120
Let Your Living Water Flow	720
Let's Worship	250
Living below in this old sinful world	356
Lo! What a Glorious Sight	416
Lord God Almighty	601
Lord, I Thank You	600
Lord I Want to Thank You	248
Lord of All	203
Lord, Speak to Me	477
Lord, We Come Before Thee Now	415
Lord, we sing your praises loud	202
Love Lifted Me	414
Love, Love, Love	723, 913
Love the Lord	249
Low in the Grave He Lay	469
Make Me a Channel of Your Peace	388
"Man of Sorrows!" what a name	450
Matthew, Mark, Luke, John	924
Men Who Dream	204
Mercy	251
Mercy Lord	252
Mine eyes have seen the glory	458, 802
Much More Than Gold	254
My God and I	467
My God Is So Great	916
My Heart and My Passion	259
My Heart Rejoices	257
My Hope Is Built	463
My Jesus, I Love Thee	371
My Rock	253
My Soul Glorifies the Lord	256
My soul! Oh, my soul finds rest	803
Nearer, Still Nearer	404
No Other Love	258

Title	Page
No Tears in Heaven	408
O Come, All Ye Faithful	550
O Come, O Come, Emmanuel	551
O Holy God	205
O I need your love in this shadowed place	218
O Increase My Love	200
O land of rest, for thee I sigh!	389
O Lord, Almighty King, praise and honor we shall sing	211
O Lord, my God! When I in awesome wonder	387
O Lord, Our Lord (How Excellent Thy Name)	110
O Lord prepare me	440
O Master, Let Me Walk with Thee	413
O Praise the Lord	108
O Rock of Ages	265
O Sacred Head	409
O Se	263
O Worship the King	438
Oh, Be Careful	915
Oh, How I Love Jesus	726
On a hill far away stood an old rugged cross	358
On Zion's Glorious Summit	412
Only God	261
Onward, Christian Soldiers	406
Oo—O—Lord we magnify your name	201
Open My Eyes	260
Our God	262
Our God, He Is Alive	351
Our God is an awesome God	445
Peace Like a River	920
Peace, Perfect Peace	374
Praise God	105
Praise Him! Praise Him! (Traditional)	379
Praise Him, Praise Him	919
Praise the Lord	107
Praise the Lord O My Soul (Craig)	116
Praise the Lord O My Soul (Golland)	118
Praises Heard Around the World	264
Pray for the Peace of Jerusalem	219
Prayer for Boldness	210
Precious Lord	364
Psalm 117	117
Purer in Heart	405
Redeemed	401
Rejoice in the Law of the Lord!	109
Rejoice in the Lord Always	111, 918
Remember Me	208
Ring Out the Message	403
Rise and Shine	922
Rise Up, O Men of God	384
Roll the Gospel Chariot	917
Run to the Fight	602
Sanctuary	440
See the little baby, lying in the manger	701
Seek Ye First	446
Send the Light	369
Set Apart	269
Shake the Earth	270
Shall We Gather at the River?	373
Shine	267
Shout for Joy	106
Show Me the Way	925
Show Me the Wonder	266
Sign Me Up	728
Siku Rin Wana (One of These Days)	603
Silent Night	556
Sing Amen, Amen	727
Sing and Rejoice	268
Sing Hallelujah to the Lord	441
Sing My Way Home	271
Sing of His Righteousness	272
Sing the wondrous love of Jesus	397
Soldiers of Christ, Arise!	444
Some glad morning when this life is o'er	422
Someday	730
Sometimes I feel that I could fight an army	209
Song of Moses	275
Soon and Very Soon	731
Spirit of the Living God	402
Stand Defiant	276
Stand in Awe	213
Stand Up, Stand Up for Jesus	400
Standin' in the Need of Prayer	923
Standing on the Promises	355
Strong in Spirit	278
Strong in the Grace	277
Surefooted	286
Surrendered	284
Sweet is the song	401
Sweet, Sweet Spirit	353
Swing Low, Sweet Chariot	732
Take a Look on the Mountain	207
Take My Life, and Let It Be	354
Take the Lord with You	733
Teach Me, Lord, to Wait	455
Ten Thousand Angels	377
Thank You, Lord	700
Thank You, Lord (Craig)	212
The blind man sat by the road and he cried	925
The Christian Jubilee	914
The Glory-Land Way	399
The Glory Song	604
The Goodness of the Lord	282
The house of the Lord	219
The Law of the Lord	101
The Lord Almighty is with us	2
The Lord Bless You and Keep You	396
The Lord is mine and I am his	905
The Lord's My Shepherd	114
The New Testament Song	924
The Old Rugged Cross	358
The Power	247
The Sea of Galilee	926
The Spacious Firmament on High	394
The Spirit's Fire	273
The Steadfast Love of the Lord	102
The Wise Man	929
The wise man built his house upon the rock	929
Come and go with me to my Father's house	911
There Is a Balm in Gilead	724
There Is a Habitation	363
There is a name I love to hear	726
There Is a Place of Quiet Rest	393
There is, beyond the azure blue	351
There Is Much to Do	381

Title	Page
There's a call comes ringing o'er the restless waves	396
There's a Fountain Free	447
There's a message true and glad	403
There's Not a Friend	435
There's Power in the Blood	350
They bound the hands of Jesus	377
They tried my Lord and Master	420
This Is My Commandment	928
This Is My Father's World	391
This Is the Day	927
This Little Light of Mine	908
This World Is Not My Home	383
Though we are free from all men	801
Time is filled with swift transition	367
'Tis Midnight and on Olive's Brow	411
To Canaan's Land I'm on My Way	392
To God Be the Glory	375
Trials dark on every hand	410
Trouble come my way	719
Trust and Obey	427
Unshakable Faith	280
Unto Thee, O Lord	100
Victory in Jesus	357
Wade in the Water	734
Walking on the Heaven Road	739
Walking in sunlight, all of my journey	428
We Are Soldiers in the Army	901
We Make it Our Goal to Please Him	274
We Praise Thee, O God	461
We Shall Overcome	736
We Will Glorify	378
We'll Work till Jesus Comes	389
Well, the war began in 'seventy-nine	604
We're Marching to Zion	459
Were You There?	735
What a Fellowship	385
What a Friend We Have in Jesus	390
What Can Wash Away My Sin?	380
What Child Is This?	555
When I Survey the Wondrous Cross	382
When Jesus gathered the twelve disciples	208
When My Love to Christ Grows Weak	457
When peace like a river	456
When the Morning Comes	410
When the Morning Comes (Fawcett)	281
When the Roll Is Called	365
When the Savior calls, I will answer	717
When the trumpet of the Lord shall sound	365
When We All Get to Heaven	397
When we walk with the Lord	427
Where Could I Go?	356
White As Snow	279
Who's that walkin' down the road	739
Whose Side Are You Fightin' On?	921
Why Did My Savior Come to Earth?	398
Why should I feel discouraged?	713
Would you be free from your burden of sin?	350
Would You Be Poured Out Like Wine?	738
Years I Spent in Vanity and Pride	386
You said you'd come and share all my sorrows	362
Your Name	285
Your Ways	283

Topical Index

Baptism
- All to Jesus I Surrender 474
- For Those Tears, I Died 362
- I Have Decided to Follow Jesus 716
- Just As I Am 471
- Lead Me to Calvary 429
- My Jesus, I Love Thee 371
- Nearer, Still Nearer 404
- Redeemed 401
- Seek Ye First 446
- There's Power in the Blood 350

Bible/Word of God
- Hallelujah 202
- How Firm a Foundation 443
- I Love Your Word 246
- In the Kingdom 605
- Jesus Loves Me! 424
- Rejoice in the Law of the Lord! 109
- Standing on the Promises 355
- The Law of the Lord 101
- The New Testament Song 924
- Trust and Obey 427
- Where Could I Go? 356

Birth of Christ
- Angels We Have Heard on High 554
- Hark! The Herald Angels Sing 557
- It Came upon a Midnight Clear 553
- Joy to the World 552
- O Come, All Ye Faithful 550
- O Come, O Come, Emmanuel 551
- Silent Night 556
- What Child Is This? 555

Blessing
- All to Jesus I Surrender 474
- Blessed Assurance 451
- God Moves in a Mysterious Way 361
- He's On Time 606
- I Walk with the King 426
- Lord, We Come Before Thee Now 415
- Praise God 105
- Ring Out the Message 403
- Seek Ye First 446
- Sing My Way Home 271
- Sweet, Sweet Spirit 353
- Thank You, Lord 212
- The Lord Bless You and Keep You 396

Blood of Christ
- Arise, My Soul, Arise 473
- Blessed Assurance 451
- Glory Be to Jesus 366
- Hallelujah 202
- Hallelujah! What a Savior! 450
- I've Been Redeemed 725
- Just As I Am 471
- Lamb of God 417
- My Hope Is Built 463
- Nearer, Still Nearer 404
- On Zion's Glorious Summit 412
- Take a Look on the Mountain 207
- Thank You, Lord (New) 700
- There's Pow'r in the Blood 350
- To God Be the Glory 375
- Victory in Jesus 357
- What Can Wash Away My Sin? 380
- When I Survey the Wondrous Cross 382

Church
- Always Triumphant 211
- For the Beauty of the Earth 470
- Great Among the Nations 206
- Hallelujah 202
- Onward, Christian Soldiers 406
- Rise up, O Men of God 384
- The Glory Song 604
- What a Fellowship 385

Comfort
- Abide with Me 478
- Anchor For the Soul 223
- Be Still, My Soul 465
- For Those Tears, I Died 362
- His Hands 241
- In My Father's House 911
- It Is Well with My Soul 456
- Jesus Is Lord 423
- Lord of All 203
- Nearer, Still Nearer 404
- No Tears in Heaven 408
- Peace, Perfect Peace 374
- Precious Lord 364
- Show Me The Wonder 266
- The Lord's My Shepherd 114
- There Is a Place of Quiet Rest 393

Communion/Cross
- Abba Father 221
- Alas! And Did My Savior Bleed? 431
- Amazing Grace 359, 800
- Beneath the Cross of Jesus 454
- Blessed Assurance 451
- Christ, the Lord, Is Risen Today 452
- Christ, We Do All Adore Thee 475
- Crown Him with Many Crowns 437
- Eloi 227
- Follow Me 439
- For Those Tears, I Died 362
- Glory Be to Jesus 366
- Hallelujah! What a Savior! 450
- It Is Well with My Soul 456
- Jesus Is Lord 423
- Jesus, Keep Me near the Cross 419
- Lamb of God 417
- Lead Me to Calvary 429
- Let Us Break Bread Together 721
- Low in the Grave He Lay 469
- My Jesus, I Love Thee 371
- Nearer, Still Nearer 404
- O Sacred Head 409
- Remember Me 208
- Sing Hallelujah to the Lord 441
- Take a Look on the Mountain 207
- Ten Thousand Angels 377
- The Old Rugged Cross 358
- There's a Fountain Free 447
- 'Tis Midnight and on Olive's Brow 411
- Were You There? 735
- When I Survey the Wondrous Cross 382
- When My Love to Christ Grows Weak 457
- Why Did My Savior Come to Earth? 398
- Would You Be Poured Out Like Wine? 738

Confession
- Beneath the Cross of Jesus 454
- Humble Yourself in the Sight of the Lord .. 104

Courage
- A Mighty Fortress 360
- Always Triumphant 211
- Be Still and Know I Am God 2
- Be Strong, Take Heart 220
- Be with Me, Lord 209
- Glory, Glory, Hallelujah! 458, 802
- God Moves in a Mysterious Way 361
- I Am Not Afraid 112
- I Hear God Singing to Me 217
- I'm Not Ashamed to Own My Lord 460
- Onward, Christian Soldiers 406
- Prayer for Boldness 210
- Ring Out the Message 403

Rise Up, O Men of God 384
Show Me The Wonder 266
Sing and Rejoice 268
Soldiers of Christ, Arise! 444
Stand Up, Stand Up for Jesus 400
The Glory Song 604
We Are Soldiers in the Army 901

Creation
Ain't No Rock 900
Fairest Lord Jesus 453
For the Beauty of the Earth 470
Great Is Thy Faithfulness 436
Hallelujah! Praise Jehovah! 433
Have You Not Heard? 3
Holy, Holy, Holy 442
How Great Thou Art 387
Immortal, Invisible, God Only Wise 407
Joy to the World 552
Joyful, Joyful, We Adore Thee 464
My God Is So Great 916
Our God, He Is Alive 351
Praise God 105
Praise the Lord 107
Stand in Awe 213
The Spacious Firmament on High 394
This Is My Father's World 391

Discipleship
A Faithful Witness 222
Crossing Over 702
Deep Down in My Heart 903
Follow Me 439
Go and Make Disciples 214
I Am Resolved 372
I Have Decided to Follow Jesus 716
If You Want to Love Him 610
I'll Be a Friend to Jesus 420
Lord, Speak to Me 477
O Master, Let Me Walk with Thee 413
Rise Up, O Men of God 384
Seek Ye First 446
Set Apart 269
Shine 267
Take the Lord with You 733
The Glory Song 604
We Make It Our Goal to Please Him 274
Whose Side Are You Fightin' On? 921

Encouragement
A Mighty Fortress 360
Amazing Grace 359, 800
Blessed Assurance 451
Encourage My Soul 704
Follow Me 439
God Alone 803
God Moves in a Mysterious Way 361
Great Is Thy Faithfulness 436
Have You Not Heard? 3
He's On Time 606
How Firm a Foundation 443
I Know That My Redeemer Lives 462
I Love to Tell the Story 418
I'm Gonna View That Holy City 909
It Is Well with My Soul 456
Lo! What a Glorious Sight 416
My Hope Is Built 463
Peace, Perfect Peace 374
Soon and Very Soon 731
Stand Up, Stand Up for Jesus 400
The Glory Song 604
The Goodness of the Lord 282
There Is a Balm in Gilead 724
There's Not a Friend 435
Trust and Obey 427
Walking on the Heaven Road 739
We Shall Overcome 736
What a Friend We Have in Jesus 390

When We All Get to Heaven 397

Faith
Alas! And Did My Savior Bleed? 431
By Faith 225
Faith Is the Victory 434
God Alone 803
How Firm a Foundation 443
I Know That My Redeemer Lives (Messiah) 376
I Know Whom I Have Believed 425
Lo! What a Glorious Sight 416
Make Me a Channel of Your Peace 388
Men Who Dream 204
My God Is So Great 916
Standing on the Promises 355
Teach Me, Lord, to Wait 455
Unshakable Faith 280
We Shall Overcome 736
When My Love to Christ Grows Weak 457

Fellowship
Amazing Grace 359, 800
Crossing Over 702
For the Beauty of the Earth 470
How Sweet, How Heavenly 370
I Hear God Singing to Me 217
In the Kingdom 605
Joyful, Joyful, We Adore Thee 464
Let Us Break Bread Together 721
Men Who Dream 204
No Tears in Heaven 408
Onward, Christian Soldiers 406
Praise Heard Around the World 264
Run to the Fight 602
Take the Lord with You 733
The Glory Song 604
This Is My Commandment 928
What a Fellowship 385
When We All Get to Heaven 397
Where Could I Go? 356

Forgiveness
Great Is Thy Faithfulness 436
I'm Happy Today 907
I've Been Redeemed 725
Make Me a Channel of Your Peace 388
Mercy 251
Mercy Lord 252
Sing My Way Home 271
There's Power in the Blood 350
This World Is Not My Home 383
Unto Thee, O Lord 100
What Can Wash Away My Sin? 380
White As Snow 279
Years I Spent in Vanity and Pride 386

God
Awesome God 445
Be Still and Know I Am God 2
God Almighty Reigns 216
God Alone 803
God Alone is Good 115
God Is So Good 706
God Moves in a Mysterious Way 361
God of Our Fathers 368
Great Is Thy Faithfulness 436
Hallelujah Chorus 880
How Great Thou Art 387
I Hear God Singing to Me 217
My God and I 467
My God Is So Great 916
Our God, He Is Alive 351
Sing of His Righteousness 272
The Goodness of the Lord 282
To God Be the Glory 375

Gospel
Entrusted 228
Love, Love, Love 723, 913
Ring Out the Message 403

Roll the Gospel Chariot 917
Send the Light 369
Stand Up, Stand Up for Jesus 400
The Glory-Land Way 399
We Are Soldiers in the Army 901

Grace and Love of God
Alas! And Did My Savior Bleed? 431
Amazing Grace 359, 800
Glorious Things of Thee Are Spoken 352
He Gave Her Water 707
His Banner over Me Is Love 905
His Love Endures Forever 4
Humble Yourself in the Sight of the Lord ... 104
I Know Whom I Have Believed 425
I Love to Tell the Story 418
I Need Your Love 218
I've Got the Joy, Joy, Joy 912
Joy to the World 552
Lord, I Thank You 600
Love Lifted Me 414
Love, Love, Love 723, 913
Make Me a Channel of Your Peace 388
Much More Than Gold 254
My Heart and My Passion 259
No Other Love 258
O Holy God 205
O Increase My Love 200
O Praise the Lord 108
Remember Me 208
Strong in the Grace 277
The Lord Bless You and Keep You 396
The Steadfast Love of the Lord 102
We Praise Thee, O God 461
When I Survey the Wondrous Cross 382
When We All Get to Heaven 397
Why Did My Savior Come to Earth? 398
Years I Spent in Vanity and Pride 386

Gratitude/Celebration
Amazing Grace 359, 800
God Almighty Reigns 216
God of Our Fathers 368
Greater Worth Than Gold 237
I Can't Keep It to Myself 712
I Feel Good 714
I Love to Tell the Story 418
I Tried and I Tried 737, 906
I Will Sing the Wondrous Story 449
I'm Happy Today 907
I've Been Redeemed 725
Kyrie Eleison (Lord, Have Mercy) 201
Lord, I Thank You 600
Lord I Want to Thank You 248
My Soul Glorifies The Lord 256
O Holy God 205
Praise the Lord O My Soul (Craig) 116
Praise the Lord O My Soul (Golland) 118
Rejoice in the Law of the Lord! 109
Rejoice in the Lord Always 111, 918
Siku Rin Wana (One of These Days) 603
Thank You, Lord 212
Thank You, Lord (New) 700
This Is the Day 927
Walking on the Heaven Road 739
White As Snow 279

Guidance
Abide with Me 478
God Moves in a Mysterious Way 361
God of Our Fathers 368
God Will Do Everything 236
Great Is Thy Faithfulness 436
Higher Ground 240
I Want Jesus to Walk with Me 715
Just a Closer Walk with Thee 472
Lord, We Come Before Thee Now 415
O Holy God 205

Open My Eyes 260
Purer in Heart 405
Run to the Fight 602
Seek Ye First 446
Thank You, Lord 212
The Lord's My Shepherd 114
The Spirit's Fire 273
There's Not a Friend 435

Heart
Abba Father 221
Breathe on Me, Breath of God 468
Cornerstone 226
Create in Me a Pure Heart 1, 804
Deep Down in My Heart 903
Glory, Glory, Hallelujah! 458, 802
I've Got the Joy, Joy, Joy 912
Purer in Heart 405
Take My Life, and Let It Be 354

Heaven/Eternal Life
Abide with Me 478
Breathe on Me, Breath of God 468
Don't You Wanna Go? 705
Glorious Things of Thee Are Spoken 352
Home in Heaven 607
Home With You 239
I Am a Poor, Wayfaring Stranger 710
I Know That My Redeemer Lives 462
I Walk with the King 426
I'll Fly Away 422
I'm Building Me a Home 608
I'm Coming Up, Lord 718
I'm Gonna View That Holy City 909
In the Kingdom 605
Jordan River 729
Kyrie Eleison (Lord, Have Mercy) 201
Lo! What a Glorious Sight 416
My God and I 467
My Jesus, I Love Thee 371
No Tears in Heaven 408
On Zion's Glorious Summit 412
Shall We Gather at the River? 373
Soon and Very Soon 731
Swing Low, Sweet Chariot 732
Thank You, Lord (New) 212
The Glory-Land Way 399
The Glory Song 604
There Is a Habitation 363
This World Is Not My Home 383
To Canaan's Land I'm on My Way 392
Victory in Jesus 357
Wade in the Water 734
Walking on the Heaven Road 739
We're Marching to Zion 459
When the Morning Comes 410
When the Morning Comes (Fawccett) 281
When the Roll Is Called 365
When We All Get to Heaven 397

Holiness
Higher Ground 240
Holy Father 395
Holy, Holy, Holy 442
Holy is The Lord 242
Holy Perfect Always Forever 243
I Know That My Redeemer Lives (Messiah) 376
O Holy God 205
On Zion's Glorious Summit 412
Purer in Heart 405
Sanctuary 440
We Make It Our Goal to Please Him 274

Holy Spirit
Arise, My Soul, Arise 473
I Feel Good 714
I Hear God Singing to Me 217
Let Your Living Water Flow 720
Praise God 105

Spirit of the Living God 402
Stand in Awe 213
Strong in Spirit 278
Sweet, Sweet Spirit 353
The Spirit's Fire 273
There Is a Balm in Gilead 724

Hope
Abide with Me 478
Blessed Assurance 451
Even Greater Things 229
Great Is Thy Faithfulness 436
Have You Not Heard? 3
Hold to God's Unchanging Hand 367
I'll Fly Away 422
I'm Gonna View That Holy City 909
Lo! What a Glorious Sight 416
Make Me a Channel of Your Peace 388
Men Who Dream 204
My God and I 467
My Hope Is Built 463
Remember Me 208
Soon and Very Soon 731
Swing Low, Sweet Chariot 732
Thank You, Lord (New) 212
The Steadfast Love of the Lord 102
There's a Fountain Free 447
To Canaan's Land I'm on My Way 392
Wade in the Water 734

Humility
All to Jesus I Surrender 474
How Great Thou Art 387
Humble Yourself in the Sight of the Lord ... 104
I Need Thee Every Hour 430
Lord, I Thank You 600
Lord, We Come Before Thee Now 415
Spirit of the Living God 402
We Will Glorify 378
When I Survey the Wondrous Cross 382
Years I Spent in Vanity and Pride 386
Your Ways 283

Invitation
All to Jesus I Surrender 474
Have Thine Own Way 432
I Am Resolved 372
Just As I Am 471
Lord, We Come Before Thee Now 415
Spirit of the Living God 402
Take My Life, and Let It Be 354
There's a Fountain Free 447
There's Power in the Blood 350
Trust and Obey 427

Jesus
All Hail the Power 476, 881
All to Jesus I Surrender 474
Amen 701
Christ, the Lord, Is Risen Today 452
Christ, We Do All Adore Thee 475
Cornerstone 226
Fairest Lord Jesus 453
Glory Be to Jesus 366
Hallelujah 202
Hallelujah! What a Savior! 450
Jesus Will Fix It 719
Jesus Is Lord 423, 805
Jesus Loves Me! 424
Jesus Loves the Little Children 910
Lamb of God 417
Lord of All 203
Low in the Grave He Lay 469
My Jesus, I Love Thee 371
O Sacred Head 409
O Se 263
Oh, How I Love Jesus 726
Ten Thousand Angels 377
There's Not a Friend 435

'Tis Midnight and on Olive's Brow 411
We Praise Thee, O God 461
What a Friend We Have in Jesus 390
Your Name 285

Kingdom
Building up the Kingdom 932
For All Generations 234
Great Among the Nations 206
I Am Resolved 372
In the Kingdom 605
Seek Ye First 446
The Glory Song 604
What a Fellowship 385

Lordship
All Hail the Power 476, 881
Fairest Lord Jesus 453
Feed My Sheep 232
Hallelujah 202
Hallelujah Chorus 880
Have You Not Heard? 3
He Is Lord! 709
I Have Decided to Follow Jesus 716
Jesus Is Lord 423, 805
Joy to the World 552
Kyrie Eleison (Lord, Have Mercy) 201
Lord of All 203
Low in the Grave He Lay 469
Much More Than Gold 254
O Lord, Our Lord 110
Shine 267
Take a Look on the Mountain 207
This Is My Father's World 391
We Will Glorify 378

Obedience
Go and Make Disciples 214
Have Thine Own Way 432
How Majestic Is Your Name 113
I Am Resolved 372
I Have Decided to Follow Jesus 716
I Will Speak 466
I'll Be a Friend to Jesus 420
I'm Coming Up, Lord 718
Purer in Heart 405
Stand Up, Stand Up for Jesus 400
Take My Life, and Let It Be 354
Ten Thousand Angels 377
The Glory-Land Way 399
'Tis Midnight and on Olive's Brow 411
Trust and Obey 427
Victory in Jesus 357
Would You Be Poured Out Like Wine? 738

Peace
Abide with Me 478
Be Still, My Soul 465
Blessed Assurance 451
Great Is Thy Faithfulness 436
His Eye Is on the Sparrow 713
Holy Father 395
In My Father's House 911
It Is Well with My Soul 456
Love, Love, Love 723, 913
Make Me a Channel of Your Peace 388
O Come, O Come, Emmanuel 551
O Increase My Love 200
O Master, Let Me Walk with Thee 413
Peace Like a River 920
Peace, Perfect Peace 374
Pray for the Peace of Jerusalem 219
The Lord Bless You and Keep You 396
The Lord's My Shepherd 114
There Is a Place of Quiet Rest 393

Persecution
Abide with Me 478
Be Still and Know I Am God 2
Be Still, My Soul 465

Be Strong, Take Heart 220
I Am Resolved 372
I Hear God Singing to Me 217
I'm Not Ashamed to Own My Lord 460
On Zion's Glorious Summit 412
Ten Thousand Angels 377
The Glory Song 604

Perseverance
Encourage My Soul 704
Finish this Race 231
Have You Not Heard? 3
I Have Decided to Follow Jesus 716
O Sacred Head 409
Strong in the Spirit 277
Teach Me, Lord, to Wait 455
We Shall Overcome 736
When My Love to Christ Grows Weak........457

Power of God
A Mighty Fortress 360
A Stream in the Desert 215
All Hail the Power 476, 881
Always Triumphant 211
Awesome God 445
Be Still and Know I Am God 2
Glory, Glory, Hallelujah! 458, 802
God Almighty Reigns 216
God Alone 803
Hallelujah 202
Low in the Grave He Lay 469
My God Is So Great 916
My Rock 253
O Holy God 205
Our God 262
Our God, He Is Alive 351
Praise the Lord 107
Shake the Earth 270
Sing Hallelujah to the Lord 441
Soldiers of Christ, Arise! 444
Song of Moses 275
Stand in Awe 213
Ten Thousand Angels 377
The Glory Song 604
The Power 247

Praise/Worship
A Stream in the Desert 215
Ain't No Rock 900
All Hail the Power 476, 881
Always Triumphant 211
Angels We Have Heard on High 554
Awesome God 445
Blessed Assurance 451
Christ, the Lord, Is Risen Today 452
Christ, We Do All Adore Thee 475
Crown Him with Many Crowns 437
For the Beauty of the Earth 470
Glorious Things of Thee Are Spoken 352
Glory Be to Jesus 366
God Almighty Reigns 216
God Moves in a Mysterious Way 361
God of Our Fathers 368
Great Is Thy Faithfulness 436
Hallelujah 202
Hallelujah Chorus 880
Hallelujah! Praise Jehovah! 433
Hallelujah! What a Savior! 450
Hark! The Herald Angels Sing 557
His Love Endures Forever 4
Holy, Holy, Holy 442
How Great Thou Art 387
Holy is The Lord 242
Holy Perfect Always Forever 243
How Majestic Is Your Name 113
I Love to Praise His Holy Name 722
I The Created 245
I Will Call upon the Lord 103

I'm Gonna Praise You 609
Immortal, Invisible, God Only Wise 407
Joyful, Joyful We Adore Thee 464
Let Us Break Bread Together 721
Lord, I Thank You 600
Low in the Grave He Lay 469
My Heart Rejoices 257
O Come, All Ye Faithful 550
O Holy God 205
O Lord, Our Lord 110
O Praise the Lord 108
O Rock of Ages 265
O Worship the King 438
On Zion's Glorious Summit 412
Onward, Christian Soldiers 406
Praise God 105
Praise Heard Around the World 264
Praise Him! Praise Him! 379, 919
Praise the Lord 107
Praise the Lord O My Soul (Craig) 116
Praise the Lord O My Soul (Golland) 118
Psalm 117 117
Shout for Joy 106
Sing and Rejoice 268
Sing Hallelujah to the Lord 441
Stand in Awe 213
The Spacious Firmament on High 394
To God Be the Glory 375
We Praise Thee, O God 461
We Will Glorify 378

Prayer
Abide with Me 478
Be Strong, Take Heart 220
Be with Me, Lord 209
Breathe on Me, Breath of God 468
Create in Me a Pure Heart 1, 804
I Need Your Love 218
I've Been Redeemed 725
Jesus Will Fix It 719
Just a Closer Walk with Thee 472
Just a Little Talk with Jesus 448
Lead Me to Some Soul Today 421
Lead Me to The Rock 119
Nearer, Still Nearer 404
O Holy God 205
O Increase My Love 200
O Master, Let Me Walk with Thee 413
Pray for the Peace of Jerusalem 219
Prayer for Boldness 210
Run to the Fight 602
Sanctuary 440
Spirit of the Living God 402
Standin' in the Need of Prayer 923
Take My Life, and Let It Be 354
Teach Me, Lord, to Wait 455
The Glory Song 604
Unto Thee, O Lord 100
What a Friend We Have in Jesus 390

Promises
Anchor For the Soul 223
As For Me and My House 224
For Those Tears, I Died 362
His Love Endures Forever 4
I Will Speak 466
I'm Not Ashamed to Own My Lord 460
Just As I Am 471
Onward, Christian Soldiers 406
Standing on the Promises 355
To God Be the Glory 375

Refuge
A Mighty Fortress 360
Abide with Me 478
Be Still and Know I Am God 2
Beneath the Cross of Jesus 454
God Almighty Reigns 216

God Alone 803
How Firm a Foundation 443
In My Father's House 911
Jesus Will Fix It 719
Nearer, Still Nearer 404
Peace, Perfect Peace 374
The Lord's My Shepherd 114
There Is a Place of Quiet Rest 393
We'll Work till Jesus Comes 389
What a Friend We Have in Jesus 390
Where Could I Go? 356

Rejoicing/Joy
Amazing Grace 359, 800
Angels We Have Heard on High 554
Fill My Soul 233
Give Me Oil in My Lamp 904
Hark! The Herald Angels Sing 557
How Great Thou Art 387
I Hear God Singing to Me 217
In My Father's House 911
I've Got the Joy, Joy, Joy 912
Joy to the World 552
Joyful, Joyful, We Adore Thee 464
Let The Peoples Praise You 120
Let's Worship 250
Love, Love, Love 723, 913
Make Me a Channel of Your Peace 388
No Tears in Heaven 408
O Come, All Ye Faithful 550
O Come, O Come, Emmanuel 551
Redeemed 401
Rejoice in the Law of the Lord! 109
Rejoice in the Lord Always 111, 918
Ring Out the Message 403
Shout for Joy 106
Siku Rin Wana 603
Sing Amen, Amen 727
Thank You, Lord 700
The Glory-Land Way 399
There Is a Place of Quiet Rest 393
This Is the Day 927
To God Be the Glory 375
We're Marching to Zion 459
When We All Get to Heaven 397

Relationship with God
A Stream in the Desert 215
Abide with Me 478
Arise, My Soul, Arise 473
Be Still and Know I Am God 2
Be Still, My Soul 465
Blessed Assurance 451
Create in Me a Pure Heart 1, 804
Deeper 230
Entrusted 228
God Almighty Reigns 216
God Alone 803
Great Is Thy Faithfulness 436
His Eye Is on the Sparrow 713
Hold to God's Unchanging Hand 367
How Firm a Foundation 443
How Great Thou Art 387
Humble Yourself in the Sight of the Lord ... 104
Just a Closer Walk with Thee 472
Just a Little Talk with Jesus 448
I Need Thee Every Hour 430
I Need Your Love 218
I The Created 245
I Walk with the King 426
I Want Jesus to Walk with Me 715
I Want to Be Less 244
If You Want to Love Him 610
I'll Be a Friend to Jesus 420
Just a Closer Walk with Thee 472
Let The Light Shine Down 255
Lord, God Almighty 601

Love The Lord 249
My God and I 467
Nearer, Still Nearer 404
Oh, How I Love Jesus 726
Only God 261
Precious Lord 364
Remember Me 208
Siku Rin Wana 603
The Lord's My Shepherd 114
There Is a Place of Quiet Rest 393
When My Love to Christ Grows Weak 457

Repentance
Glory, Glory (Laid My Burdens Down) 711
I Am Resolved 372
My Jesus, I Love Thee 371
Nearer, Still Nearer 404
Remember Me 208
Victory in Jesus 357

Sacrifice
Follow Me 439
Glory, Glory, Hallelujah! 458, 802
Hallelujah! What a Savior! 450
How Great Thou Art 387
Lamb of God 417
O Holy God 205
Our God, He Is Alive 351
Show Me the Way 925
Ten Thousand Angels 377
The Glory Song 604
Victory in Jesus 357
When I Survey the Wondrous Cross 382
When My Love to Christ Grows Weak 457
Why Did My Savior Come to Earth? 398
Would You Be Poured Out Like Wine? 738

Second Coming
How Great Thou Art 387
I Know That My Redeemer Lives (Messiah) .. 376
I Know Whom I Have Believed 425
I'll Be Listening 717
I'll Fly Away 422
I'm Coming Up, Lord 718
It Is Well with My Soul 456
Jesus Is Lord 423, 805
Lo! What a Glorious Sight 416
My Hope Is Built 463
Shake the Earth 270
Sing Amen, Amen 727
Sing Hallelujah to the Lord 441
Someday 730
The Christian Jubilee 914
We'll Work till Jesus Comes 389
Why Did My Savior Come to Earth? 398

Seeking the Lost
A Faithful Witness 222
Always Triumphant 211
As Many As Possible 801
Be with Me, Lord 209
Crossing Over 702
Go and Make Disciples 214
God Almighty Reigns 216
Great Among the Nations 206
Hard Fighting Soldier 708
Here Am I Send Me 238
I Can't Keep It to Myself 712
I Hear God Singing to Me 217
I Love to Tell the Story 418
In the Kingdom 605
Lead Me to Some Soul Today 421
Lord, Speak to Me 477
Men Who Dream 204
O Increase My Love 200
Pray for the Peace of Jerusalem 219
Remember Me 208
Ring Out the Message 403
Run to the Fight 602

Send the Light	369
Show Me the Way	925
Stand in Awe	213
Take My Life, and Let It Be	354
The Glory-Land Way	399
The Glory Song	604
The Power	247
There Is a Balm in Gilead	724
There Is Much to Do	381

Serving
As For Me and My House	224
I Will Speak	466
Hard Fighting Soldier	708
Lord God Almighty	601
O Master, Let Me Walk with Thee	413
We'll Work till Jesus Comes	389
When We All Get to Heaven	397
Whose Side Are You Fightin' On?	921
Would You Be Poured Out Like Wine?	738

Singing
A Stream in the Desert	215
Always Triumphant	211
Angels We Have Heard on High	554
Be with Me, Lord	209
Blessed Assurance	451
Christ, the Lord, Is Risen Today	452
Deep Down in My Heart	903
God Almighty Reigns	216
God Alone	803
Hallelujah	202
Hark! The Herald Angels Sing	557
Have You Not Heard?	3
His Eye Is on the Sparrow	713
How Great Thou Art	387
I Hear God Singing to Me	217
I Need Your Love	218
I Will Sing the Wondrous Story	449
I'm Gonna View That Holy City	909
In the Kingdom	605
Lord God Almighty	601
Lord of All	203
Men Who Dream	204
On Zion's Glorious Summit	412
Onward, Christian Soldiers	406
Redeemed	401
Shout for Joy	106
Sing, Amen	727
Sing Hallelujah to the Lord	441
Sing of His Righteousness	272
Standing on the Promises	355
Take My Life, and Let It Be	354
The Glory Song	604
When We All Get to Heaven	397

Surrender
All to Jesus I Surrender	474
Blessed Assurance	451
Breathe on Me, Breath of God	468
Feed My Sheep	232
God Moves in a Mysterious Way	361
He Must Become Greater	235
I Want to Be Less	245
My Heart and My Passion	259
Spirit of the Living God	402
Surrendered	284
Take My Life, and Let It Be	354
Ten Thousand Angels	377

Thanksgiving
Alas! And Did My Savior Bleed?	431
Amazing Grace	359, 800
His Love Endures Forever	4
Lord, I Thank You	600
Run to the Fight	602
Thank You, Lord	212
Thank You, Lord (New)	700

Trust
Abide with Me	478
All to Jesus I Surrender	474
Blessed Assurance	451
Even Greater Things	229
For Those Tears, I Died	362
God Alone	803
God Moves in a Mysterious Way	361
He Must Become Greater	235
His Eye Is on the Sparrow	713
Hold to God's Unchanging Hand	367
Humble Yourself in the Sight of the Lord	104
I Am Not Afraid	112
Jesus Will Fix It	719
Lead Me to The Rock	119
Let Your Living Water Flow	720
My Hope Is Built	463
Standing on the Promises	355
Surefooted	286
Teach Me, Lord, to Wait	455
Trust and Obey	427
Unto Thee, O Lord	100
When the Morning Comes	410
When We All Get to Heaven	397
Your Ways	283

Victory
A Mighty Fortress	360
Abide with Me	478
Always Triumphant	211
By Faith	225
Christ, the Lord, Is Risen Today	452
Faith Is the Victory	434
God Almighty Reigns	216
Hallelujah! What a Savior!	450
Joyful, Joyful, We Adore Thee	464
Low in the Grave He Lay	469
O Holy God	205
On Zion's Glorious Summit	412
Soldiers of Christ, Arise!	444
Song of Moses	275
Stand Defiant	276
Stand in Awe	213
Stand Up, Stand Up for Jesus	400
Strong in the Grace	277
The Glory Song	604
This World Is Not My Home	383
Unshakable Faith	280
Victory in Jesus	357
We Shall Overcome	736
We're Marching to Zion	459
When the Morning Comes	410
When We All Get to Heaven	397

Zeal
Breathe on Me, Breath of God	468
Deep Down in My Heart	903
Finish this Race	231
Give Me Oil in My Lamp	904
God Almighty Reigns	216
Great Among the Nations	206
Hallelujah	202
I Hear God Singing to Me	217
Ring Out the Message	403
Run to the Fight	602
Stand Defiant	276
The Glory Song	604

Psalms

Create in Me a Pure Heart

1

Dm/D

Soprano & Tenor (tenors sing one octave lower than shown)

Cre - ate in me a pure heart God; Re - new a stead - fast spir - it

Alto & Bass (altos sing one octave higher than shown)

Cre - ate a pure heart God; Re - new my spir - it

in me. O do not cast me from Your pre - sence,

in me. O do not cast me from Your pre - sence,

Or take Your Ho - ly Spir - it from me.

p

Or take Your Ho - ly Spir - it from me.

Jubilant!
Soprano

Alto *f*

Re - store to me the joy of Your sal - va - tion, And up -

Tenor

Bass

hold me with a will - ing spir - it; Then I will

WORDS: Kevin Darby (paraphrased from Psalm 51:10-14), 1983
MUSIC: Kevin Darby, 1999
© 1998 LITA Music. Admin. by Songs for the Planet, Inc., P. O. Box 271056 Nashville, TN 37227.
All rights reserved. Used by permission.

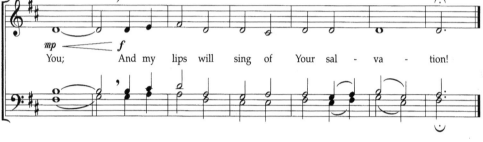

2 Be Still and Know I Am God

WORDS: Gerri Bernitt, 1999 (based on Psalm 46:7-11)
MUSIC: Gerri Bernitt, 1999
© 1999 Los Angeles International Church of Christ. All rights reserved. Used by permission.

3 Have You Not Heard?

WORDS: Brad Detrick, 1997 (paraphrase of Isaiah 40:21-31)
MUSIC: Brad Detrick, 1997
© 1997 Discipleship Publications International. All rights reserved.

His Love Endures Forever 4

WORDS: Psalm 136
MUSIC: Eric Davis, 1999
© 1999 Discipleship Publications International. All rights reserved.

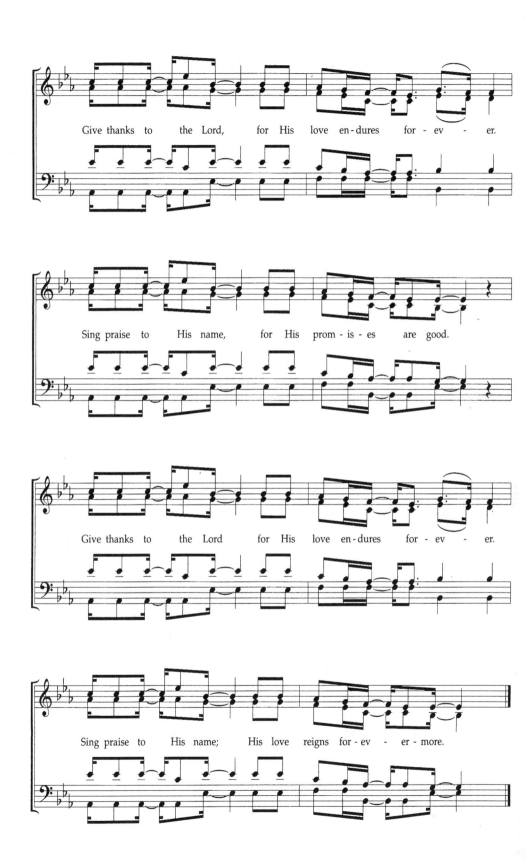

100 Unto Thee, O Lord

WORDS: Charles F. Monroe, 1971 (paraphrase of Psalm 25:1-4, 7)
MUSIC: Charles F. Monroe, 1971
© 1971 Charles Monroe Music (admin. by The Copyright Company, 40 Music Sq. E, Nashville, TN 37203).
International copyright secured. All rights reserved. Used by permission.

The Law of the Lord 101

1. The law of the Lord is perfect, converting the soul. The testimony of the Lord is sure, making wise the simple. More to be desired are they than gold, yea, than much fine gold; Sweeter also than honey and the honeycomb.
2. The statutes of the Lord are right, rejoicing the heart. The commandment of the Lord is pure, enlight'ning the eyes. More to be desired are they than gold, yea, than much fine gold; Sweeter also than honey and the honeycomb.
3. The fear of the Lord is clean, enduring forever. The judgments of the Lord are true, and righteous altogether. More to be desired are they than gold, yea, than much fine gold; Sweeter also than honey and the honeycomb.

WORDS: Psalm 19:7-11
MUSIC: Traditional spiritual

102 The Steadfast Love of the Lord

WORDS: Amy Bessire (based on Lamentations 3:22-24)
MUSIC: Amy Bessire
© 1978 Amy Bessire. International copyright secured. All rights reserved. Used by permission.

I Will Call upon the Lord 103

WORDS: Michael O'Shields, 1981 (Psalm 18:3, 46, 49)
MUSIC: Michael O'Shields, 1981
© 1981 MCA Music Publishing, a division of Universal Studios, Inc. and Sound III, Inc. All rights controlled and administered by MCA Music Publishing. International copyright secured. All rights reserved. Used by permission.

104 Humble Yourself in the Sight of the Lord

WORDS: Bob Hudson, 1978 (verse 1: 1 Peter 5:5-6, Proverbs 3:3-4; verses 2-4: by John Newton)
MUSIC: Bob Hudson, 1978

© 1978 Maranatha! Music (admin. by The Copyright Company, 40 Music Sq. E, Nashville, TN 37203).
International copyright secured. All rights reserved. Used by permission.

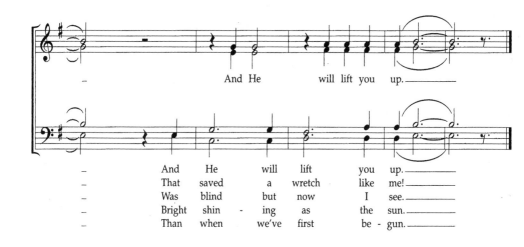

Praise God 105

WORDS: Thomas Ken, 1709 (derived from Psalm 148)
MUSIC: alt. Genevan Psalter, 1551 (Old Hundreth)

Shout for Joy

WORDS: Traditional (Psalm 100)
MUSIC: Traditional

Praise the Lord 107

1. Praise the Lord, ye heav-ens a - dore Him! Praise Him, an - gels, in the heights;
2. Praise the Lord, for He hath spo - ken; Worlds His might - y voice o - beyed;
3. Praise the Lord, for He is glo - rious; Nev - er shall His prom - ise fail;
4. Praise the God of our sal - va - tion; Hosts on high, His pow'r pro - claim;

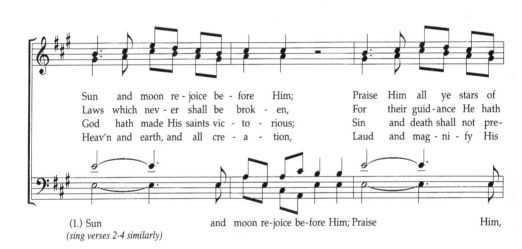

Sun and moon re - joice be - fore Him; Praise Him all ye stars of
Laws which nev - er shall be brok - en, For their guid - ance He hath
God hath made His saints vic - to - rious; Sin and death shall not pre -
Heav'n and earth, and all cre - a - tion, Laud and mag - ni - fy His

(1.) Sun and moon re-joice be-fore Him; Praise Him,
(sing verses 2-4 similarly)

light.
made.
vail.
name.

Hal - le - lu - jah! A-men, (Hal-le - lu-jah!) A-men, A-men, A - men.

all ye stars of light.

WORDS: J. Kempthorne, 1796 (Psalm 148:1-6, 13)
MUSIC: Lowell Mason, 1841

108 O Praise the Lord

WORDS: Traditional (Psalm 117)
MUSIC: Will Hill, 1921

Rejoice in the Law of the Lord! 109

First time - sopranos sing through first verse
Second time - add altos, repeat first verse
Third time - add men, repeat first verse
To end, all sing second verse in same way

WORDS: Greg Petit, 1989 (based on Psalm 1)
MUSIC: Greg Petit, 1989
© 1989 Boston Church of Christ. All rights reserved. Used by permission.

110 O Lord, Our Lord

WORDS: Horatio Palmer, 1874 (based on Psalm 8:1)
MUSIC: Horatio Palmer, 1874

111 Rejoice in the Lord Always

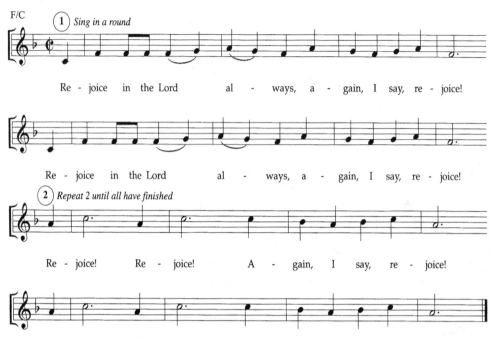

WORDS: Traditional (Philippians 4:4)
MUSIC: Traditional

112 I Am Not Afraid

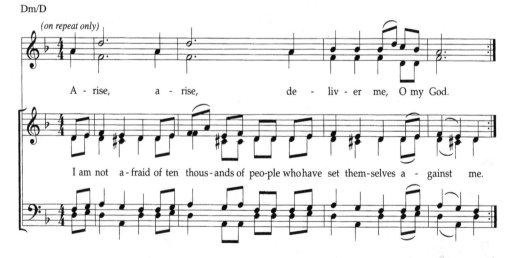

WORDS: Traditional (Psalm 3:6-7a)
MUSIC: Traditional; arr. E. Sherwin Mackintosh

How Majestic Is Your Name 113

WORDS: Michael W. Smith, 1981 (Psalm 8:1)
MUSIC: Michael W. Smith, 1981
© 1981 Meadowgreen Music Company, (ASCAP) (admin. by EMI Christian Music Pub.) International copyright secured. All rights reserved. Used by permission.

114 The Lord's My Shepherd

WORDS: Scottish Psalter, 1650 (Psalm 23)
MUSIC: John Campbell, 1854 (Orlington)

God Alone is Good 115

WORDS: Todd Gilmore (based on Psalm 73)
MUSIC: Todd Gilmore
Copyright © 2005 by Todd Gilmore. Licensed from River City Music, LLC.

117

Psalm 117

WORDS: Doug Banks
MUSIC: Doug Banks
Copyright © 2008 by Doug Banks. Licensed from River City Music, LLC.

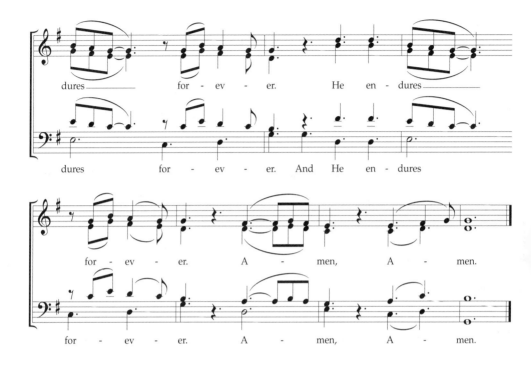

Psalms 117

[1] Praise the LORD, all you nations;
  extol him, all you peoples.
[2] For great is his love toward us,
  and the faithfulness of the LORD endures forever.

Praise the LORD.

118 Praise the Lord, O My Soul

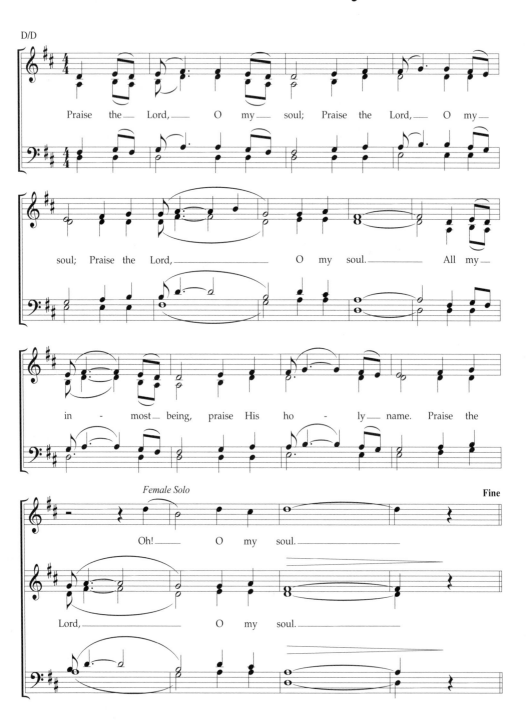

WORDS: Barish Golland
MUSIC: Barish Golland
Copyright © 2002 by Barish Golland. Licensed from River City Music, LLC.

119 Lead Me to the Rock

WORDS: J. Brian Craig. Based on Psalm 61.
MUSIC: J. Brian Craig
Copyright © 2002 by J. Brian Craig. Licensed from River City Music, LLC.

New Hymns

O Increase My Love 200

I pray, O Lord Jesus, my love you'd increase.
That I, like you, Jesus, might offer men peace.
O Jesus
My soul wells with longing for lips with Your grace and
Jesus, Jesus, Jesus, Jesus,
eyes of compassion for each searching face, face.
Jesus, Jesus, Jesus, Jesus, sus.

WORDS: T. Dorz / N. Moldoveall
MUSIC: Romanian hymn; arr. by E. Sherwin Mackintosh
© 1998 New York City Church of Christ. All rights reserved. Used by permission.

201 Kyrie Eleison
(Lord, Have Mercy)

G/G

Leader:
Oo____ O__ Lord we mag-ni-fy Your name, You spilled Your blood, we'll ne-ver be the__ same.
None but fire and__ flame, You res-cued me and gave Your pre-cious name.

Congregation:
Oo____ Oo____ Oo____

That day on Cal-va-ry you died, My pride and self-ish-ness were cru-ci-fied.
Now I stand and heed Your fi-nal call, And take Your word un-to the na-tions all.

Oo____ Oo____

1. Kyr-i-e E-le-i-son, Kyr-i-e E-le-i-son.____ De-serv-ing
   Chri-ste E-le-i-son, Chri-ste E-le-i-son.

2. continue D.S. - FINE

Kyr-i-e E-le-i-son, Kyr-i-e E-le-i-son.
Chri-ste E-le-i-son, Chri-ste E-le-i-son. Oo____

WORDS: Jon Augustine, 1998
MUSIC: Jon Augustine, 1998
© 1998 Los Angeles International Church of Christ. All rights reserved. Used by permission.

Lord of All

203

1. If life is just a song, I will sing for you.
2. Down up-on the earth to set me free;
3. Al-ways by my side, to com - fort me;
4. The world that we know will pass a-way.

(1.) If life is just a song, I will

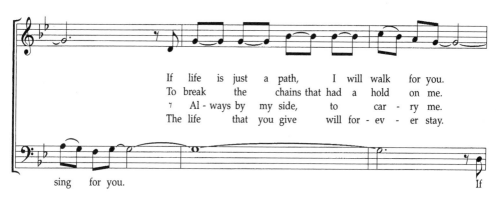

If life is just a path, I will walk for you.
To break the chains that had a hold on me.
Al - ways by my side, to car - ry me.
The life that you give will for - ev - er stay.

sing for you. If

Je - sus, Je - sus,
life is just a path, I will walk for you.

Lord of all! Je - sus, Je - sus, Lord of all!

WORDS: Larry Jackson, 1989
MUSIC: Larry Jackson, 1989
© 1989 Discipleship Publications International. All rights reserved.

204 Men Who Dream

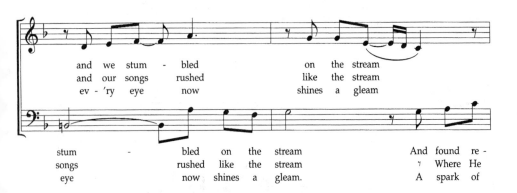

Theme Song for 1989 Boston World Missions Seminar
WORDS: Steven L. Johnson, E. Sherwin Mackintosh, Noel Scott, 1989 (based on Psalm 126)
MUSIC: Steven L. Johnson, E. Sherwin Mackintosh, Noel Scott, 1989
© 1989 New York City Church of Christ and Noel Scott. All rights reserved. Used by permission.

206 Great Among the Nations

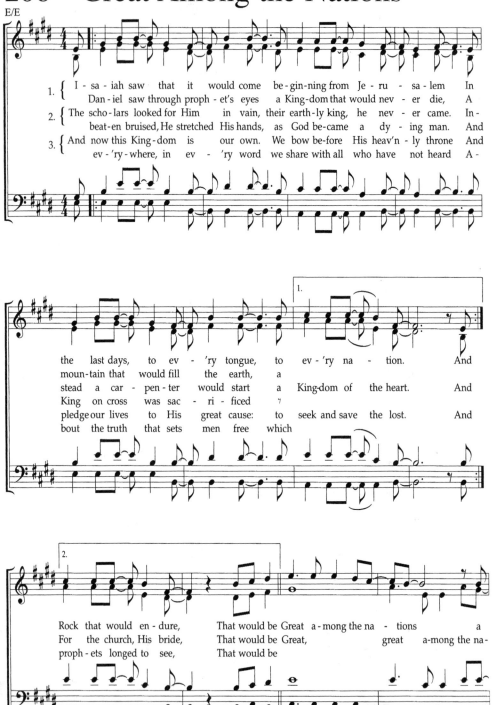

1. Isaiah saw that it would come beginning from Jerusalem In the last days, to ev'ry tongue, to ev'ry nation. And Rock that would endure, That would be Great among the nations a
2. Daniel saw through prophet's eyes a Kingdom that would never die, A mountain that would fill the earth, a Kingdom of the heart. And For the church, His bride, That would be Great, great among the na-
2. The scholars looked for Him in vain, their earthly king, he never came. Instead a carpenter would start a
   beaten bruised, He stretched His hands, as God became a dying man. And King on cross was sacrificed
   prophets longed to see, That would be
3. And now this Kingdom is our own. We bow before His heav'nly throne And pledge our lives to His great cause: to seek and save the lost. And
   ev-'ry-where, in ev-'ry word we share with all who have not heard About the truth that sets men free which

WORDS: J. Brian Craig, 1998
MUSIC: J. Brian Craig, 1998
© 1998 Discipleship Publications International. All rights reserved.

207 Take a Look on the Mountain

WORDS: Larry Jackson, 1992
MUSIC: Larry Jackson, 1992; arr. E. Sherwin Mackintosh, 1994
© 1992 Discipleship Publications International. All rights reserved.

Remember Me 208

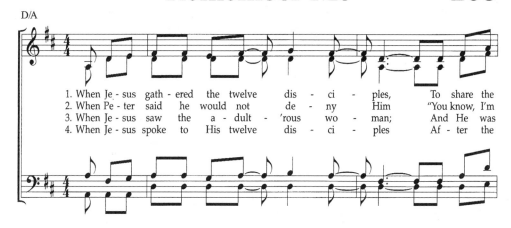

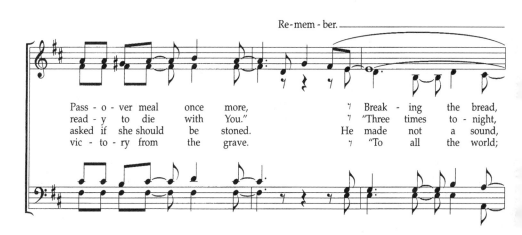

WORDS: E. Sherwin Mackintosh, 1999
MUSIC: E. Sherwin Mackintosh, 1999
© 1999 New York City Church of Christ. All rights reserved. Used by permission.

Prayer for Boldness 210

From the musical *UpsideDown*
WORDS: Steve Johnson, 1987 (based on Acts 4:23-31)
MUSIC: E. Sherwin Mackintosh, 1987
© 1987 New York City Church of Christ. All rights reserved. Used by permission.

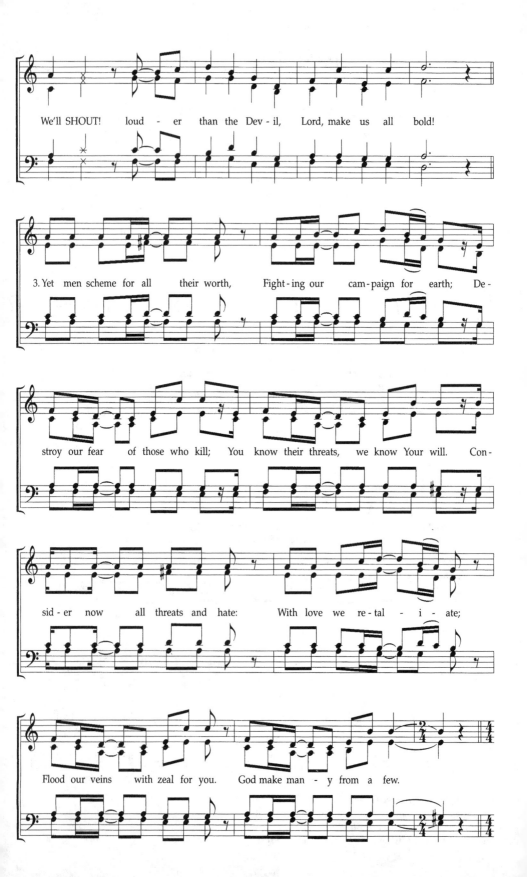

Theme song for the 1984 Boston World Missions Seminar
WORDS: Kevin Darby, 1984
MUSIC: Kevin Darby, 1984
© 1984 Boston Church of Christ. All rights reserved. Used by permission.

213 Stand in Awe

Theme song for the 1991 North American Discipleship Seminar
WORDS: Chris Guerra, 1991
MUSIC: Chris Guerra, 1991
© 1991 Chicago Church of Christ. All rights reserved. Used by permission.

Go and Make Disciples 214

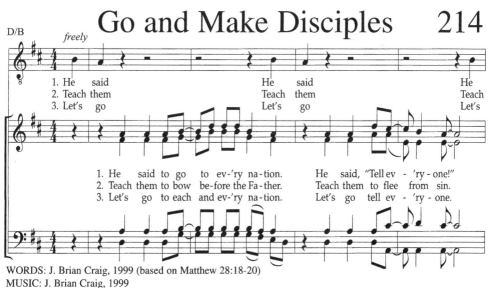

WORDS: J. Brian Craig, 1999 (based on Matthew 28:18-20)
MUSIC: J. Brian Craig, 1999
© 1999 Discipleship Publications International. All rights reserved.

A Stream in the Desert 215

1. I'm thirsty and hungry and longing, But nothing on earth can fulfill.
2. My troubles and foes can surround me. Then I call on Your name and I stand.
3. If I had ev'ry passion and pleasure, And if ease and success marked my ways,

There's a place in my heart that is empty, That only my God can fill.
I remember Your power and glory, And in praise I will lift up my hands.
Well, Your love still would be so much better than life, So my lips will keep singing Your praise.

1.&3. A stream in the desert when I'm thirsty, The richest of fare when I'm weak,
2. For I've seen You in the sanctuary. To Your presence my longing soul clings.

Thru' the darkest of nights I think only of You. Oh, Your presence I earnestly seek.
I will praise You as long as I have life to live, And I'll sing in the shadow of Your wings.

WORDS: Ashley Nelson, 1999 (based on Psalm 63)
MUSIC: Ashley Nelson, 1999
© 1999 Discipleship Publications International. All rights reserved.

217 I Hear God Singing to Me

Swahili translation by Catherine Bangeranye: "Sikiya Mungu akiimba!—Listen to God singing!"
WORDS: Steven L. Johnson, 1990 (based on Zephaniah 3:17)
MUSIC: E. Sherwin Mackintosh, 1990
© 1990 New York City Church of Christ. All rights reserved. Used by permission.

You may end the song after you return to the chorus or you may sing the Swahili section again to end the song.

The songleader may choose to raise the last chorus a whole step by modifying his pick-up to the chorus.

218 I Need Your Love

G/D

1. O I need Your love in this shadowed place;
   When it's cold and dark, or I'm far from home,
   I can't get enough of Your sunlight on my face.
   You are in my heart and I never walk alone.

2. I'm a tiny child, but when I'm with You
   Your love makes me strong though I'm small and weak,
   I will not grow tired, 'cause there's nothing You can't do.
   And the whole day long You'll speak through me when I speak.

3. You gave all for me though I'd cursed Your name;
   How can I thank You? Your love paid my way.
   On that bitter tree, Lord, You suffered for my shame.
   All that I can do is live for You ev'ry day.

And just

WORDS: J. Brian Craig, 1999
MUSIC: J. Brian Craig, 1999
© 1999 Discipleship Publications International. All rights reserved.

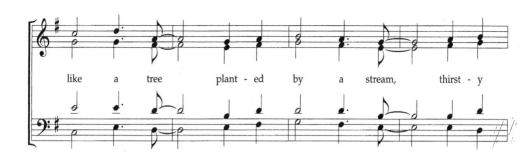

219 Pray for the Peace of Jerusalem

WORDS: J. Brian Craig, 1996 (based on Psalm 122:6-9)
MUSIC: J. Brian Craig, 1996
© 1996 Discipleship Publications International. All rights reserved.

220 Be Strong, Take Heart

WORDS: Geoff Fawcett, 1998 (based on Psalm 27)
MUSIC: Geoff Fawcett, 1998
© 1998 International Churches of Christ. All rights reserved.

Abba Father 221

WORDS: E. Sherwin Mackintosh
MUSIC: E. Sherwin Mackintosh
Copyright © 2010 by E. Sherwin Mackintosh. Licensed from River City Music, LLC.

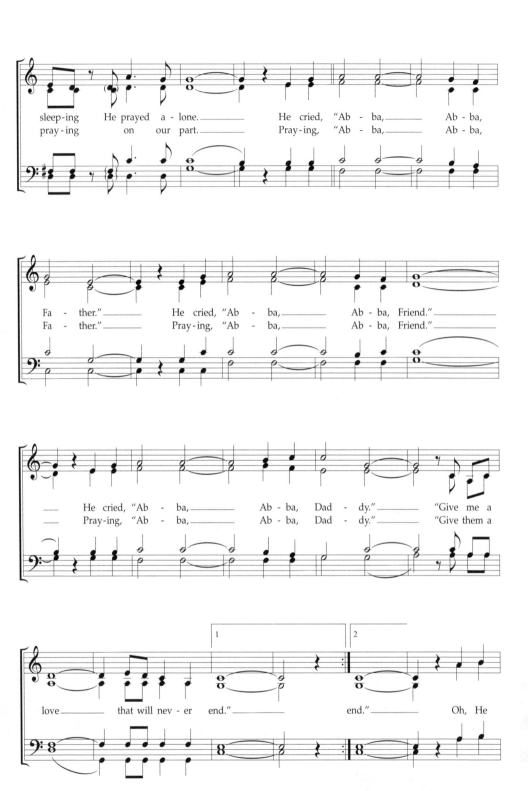

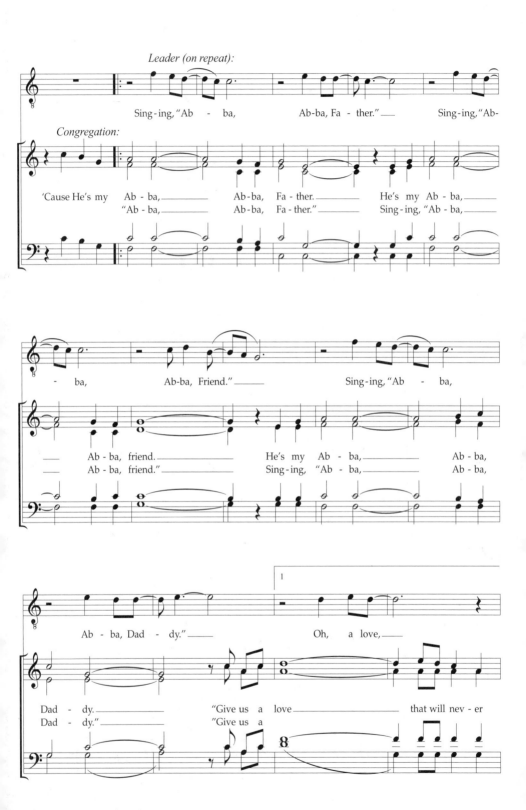

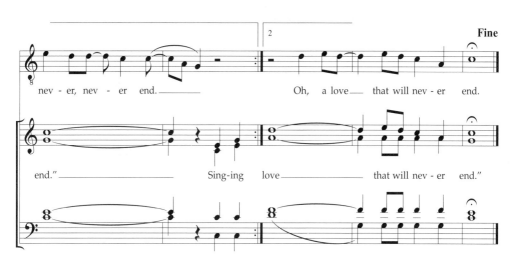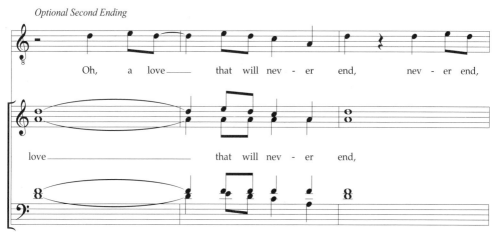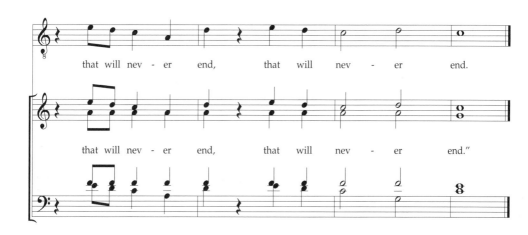

222 A Faithful Witness

WORDS: J. Brian Craig
MUSIC: J. Brian Craig
Copyright © 2008 by J. Brian Craig. Licensed from River City Music, LLC.

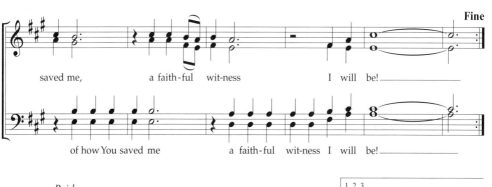

223 Anchor for the Soul

1. An-chor for the soul, shel-ter from the storm, Thun-der and the light-ning can be ver-y fright-'ning but God is in con-trol. An-chor for the soul, shel-ter from the storm, man-na in the morn-ing, bless-ings o-ver flow-ing, lead-ing us to home.

2. This world's not my home, just a pass-ing through, Through this life I wan-der, treas-ure stored up yon-der, some-where be-yond the blue. On my way I learn through each path I take. Ev-'ry day I'm grow-ing on my way I'm know-ing heav-en's worth the wait.

3. When the day is gone, when my jour-ney ends, Won't be noth-ing bet-ter than to be to-geth-er with all my faith-ful friends. We'll all join in song, gath-ered 'round the throne. There'll be no more sor-row some day when to-mor-row heav-en is our home.

WORDS: J. Brian Craig
MUSIC: J. Brian Craig
Copyright © 2008 by J. Brian Craig. Licensed from River City Music, LLC.

As For Me and My House 224

WORDS: Carol McGuirk
MUSIC: Carol McGuirk, arr. Kevin Harris
Copyright © 2008 by Carol McGuirk and Kevin Harris. Licensed from River City Music, LLC.

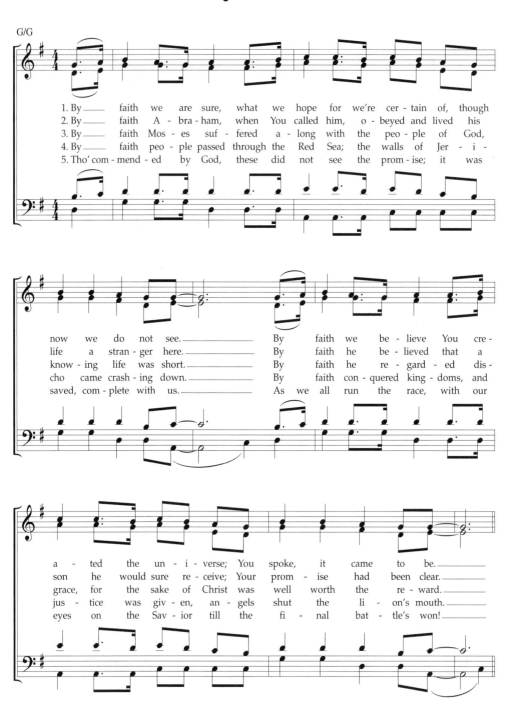

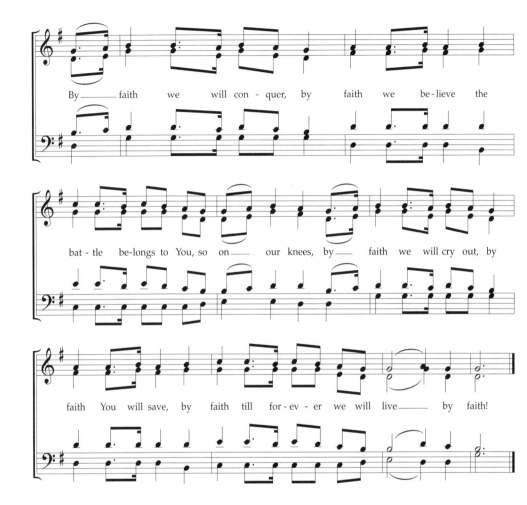

Hebrews 11:1-3

¹Now faith is confidence in what we hope for and assurance about what we do not see. ²This is what the ancients were commended for.

³By faith we understand that the universe was formed at God's command, so that what is seen was not made out of what was visible.

Cornerstone

WORDS: Mark Haven Hoyle
MUSIC: Mark Haven Hoyle
Copyright © 2005 by Mark Hoyle. Licensed from River City Music, LLC.

227 Eloi

WORDS: Gerri Bernitt
MUSIC: Gerri Bernitt
Copyright © 2006 by Gerri Bernitt. Licensed from River City Music, LLC.

229 Even Greater Things

1. Take what I've been giv - en *(Take what I've been giv - en)* make it mul - ti - ply. *(make it*
2. Gi - ant was so might - y, *(Gi - ant was so might - y,)* o - ver nine feet tall. *(o - ver*
3. It was just a peb - ble *(It was just a peb - ble)* made Go - li - ath fall. *(made Go-*

mul - ti - ply.) Take this life I'm liv - ing, *(Take this life I'm liv - ing,)* make it
nine feet tall.) Da - vid looked so ti - ny, *(Da - vid looked so ti - ny,)* seemed so
li - ath fall.) I must be more faith - ful *(I must be more faith - ful)* I must

touch the sky. *(make it touch the sky.)* You can take us high - er *(You can*
ver - y small. *(seemed so ver - y small.)* But Your hand was with him, *(But Your*
give my all. *(I must give my all.)* I've seen what You can do *(I've seen*

take us high - er) than we've ev - er been *(than we've ev - er been)* Lord, You will in - spi - re *(Lord, You*
hand was with him,) and the stone he slung. *(and the stone he slung.)* You gave him the vi - sion, *(You gave*
what You can do) with a stone and sling! *(with a stone and sling!)* Take this life I give You; *(Take this*

All sing:

will in - spi - re) Lord, You al - ways win. *(Lord, You al - ways win.)* E - ven
him the vi - sion,) and thru' You he won. *(and thru' You he won.)* E - ven
life I give You;) take my ev - 'ry - thing. *(take my ev - 'ry - thing.)* E - ven

WORDS: J. Brian Craig
MUSIC: J. Brian Craig
Copyright © 2000 by J. Brian Craig. Licensed from River City Music, LLC.

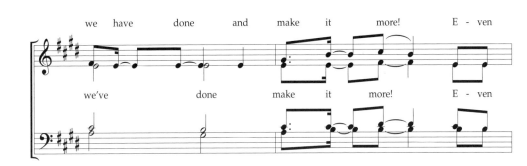

230 Deeper

WORDS: S. Chase Mackintosh
MUSIC: S. Chase Mackintosh
Copyright © 2011 by S. Chase Mackintosh. Licensed from River City Music, LLC.

Finish This Race 231

WORDS: Mark Haven Hoyle
MUSIC: Mark Haven Hoyle
Copyright © 2005 by Mark Haven Hoyle. Licensed from River City Music, LLC.

234 For All Generations

WORDS: J. Brian Craig
MUSIC: J. Brian Craig
Copyright © 2007 by J. Brian Craig. Licensed from River City Music, LLC.

He Must Become Greater   235

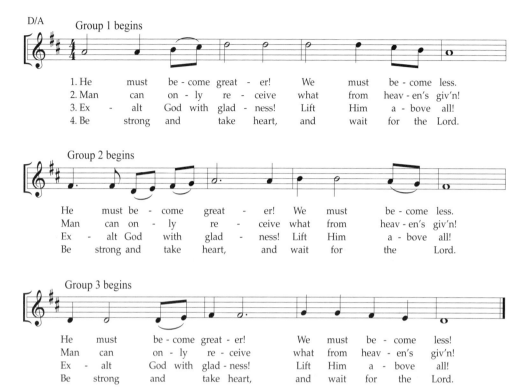

*Singers should be organized into 3 equal groups. Dynamics are up to the director's discretion. Each verse can be sung in a canon to completion before the next verse begins, or sequential verses can begin before prior verse finishes as scripture weaves together. Parts should repeat last phrase on last verse until all end together with, "and wait for the Lord!"

John 17:1-5

¹After Jesus said this, he looked toward heaven and prayed:

"Father, the time has come. Glorify your Son, that your Son may glorify you. ²For you granted him authority over all people that he might give eternal life to all those you have given him. ³Now this is eternal life: that they may know you, the only true God, and Jesus Christ, whom you have sent. ⁴I have brought you glory on earth by completing the work you gave me to do. ⁵And now, Father, glorify me in your presence with the glory I had with you before the world began."

WORDS AND MUSIC: Jerry Maday
Copyright © 2004 by Jerry Maday. Licensed from River City Music, LLC.

236 God Will Do Everything

WORDS: Mark Haven Hoyle and Beth Hoyle
MUSIC: Mark Haven Hoyle and Beth Hoyle
Copyright © 2006 by Mark HavenHoyle. Licensed from River City Music, LLC.

God will see us through. God will do ev - 'ry - thing.

Psalm 146

[1]Praise the Lord.

Praise the Lord, my soul.

[2]I will praise the Lord all my life;
   I will sing praise to my God as long as I live.
[3]Do not put your trust in princes,
   in human beings, who cannot save.
[4]When their spirit departs, they return to the ground;
   on that very day their plans come to nothing.
[5]Blessed are those whose help is the God of Jacob,
   whose hope is in the Lord their God.

[6]He is the Maker of heaven and earth,
   the sea, and everything in them—
   he remains faithful forever.
[7]He upholds the cause of the oppressed
   and gives food to the hungry.
The Lord sets prisoners free,
   [8]the Lord gives sight to the blind,
the Lord lifts up those who are bowed down,
   the Lord loves the righteous.
[9]The Lord watches over the foreigner
   and sustains the fatherless and the widow,
   but he frustrates the ways of the wicked.

[10]The Lord reigns forever,
   your God, O Zion, for all generations.

Praise the Lord.

237 Greater Worth Than Gold

WORDS: J. Brian Craig
MUSIC: J. Brian Craig
Copyright © 2005 by J. Brian Craig. Licensed from River City Music, LLC.

1 Peter 1:6-7

[6] In all this you greatly rejoice, though now for a little while you may have had to suffer grief in all kinds of trials. [7] These have come so that the proven genuineness of your faith—of greater worth than gold, which perishes even though refined by fire—may result in praise, glory and honor when Jesus Christ is revealed.

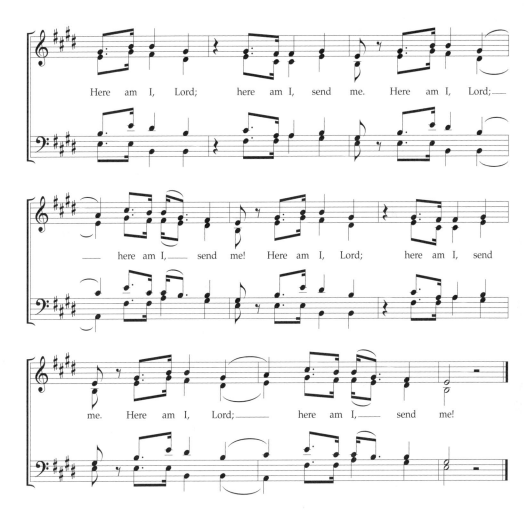

Isaiah 6:8

[8]Then I heard the voice of the Lord saying, "Whom shall I send? And who will go for us?"
 And I said, "Here am I. Send me!"

239 Home With You

WORDS: J. Brian Craig
MUSIC: J. Brian Craig
Copyright © 2005 by J. Brian Craig. Licensed from River City Music, LLC.

1 Thessalonians 4:13-18

[13]Brothers and sisters, we do not want you to be uninformed about those who sleep in death, so that you do not grieve like the rest of mankind, who have no hope. [14]For we believe that Jesus died and rose again, and so we believe that God will bring with Jesus those who have fallen asleep in him. [15]According to the Lord's word, we tell you that we who are still alive, who are left until the coming of the Lord, will certainly not precede those who have fallen asleep. [16]For the Lord himself will come down from heaven, with a loud command, with the voice of the archangel and with the trumpet call of God, and the dead in Christ will rise first. [17]After that, we who are still alive and are left will be caught up together with them in the clouds to meet the Lord in the air. And so we will be with the Lord forever. [18]Therefore encourage one another with these words.

240 Higher Ground

WORDS: Todd Gilmore
MUSIC: Todd Gilmore
Copyright © 2005 by Todd Gilmore. Licensed from River City Music, LLC.

241 His Hands

WORDS: J. Brian Craig
MUSIC: J. Brian Craig
Copyright © 2003 by J. Brian Craig. Licensed from River City Music, LLC.

243 Holy Perfect Always Forever

WORDS: Ross Lippencott
MUSIC: Ross Lippencott
Copyright © 2011 by Ross Lippencott/NYCOC. Licensed from River City Music, LLC.

I Want To Be Less

244

Psalm 50:1-2
A psalm of Asaph

[1]The Mighty One, God, the Lord,
   speaks and summons the earth
   from the rising of the sun to where it sets.
[2]From Zion, perfect in beauty,
   God shines forth.

WORDS: Ayo Owudunni
MUSIC: Ayo Owudunni
Copyright © 2008 by Ayo Owudunni. Licensed from River City Music, LLC.

245 I, The Created

WORDS: Marcus Johnson
MUSIC: Marcus Johnson
Copyright © 2009 by Marcus A. Johnson. Licensed from River City Music, LLC.

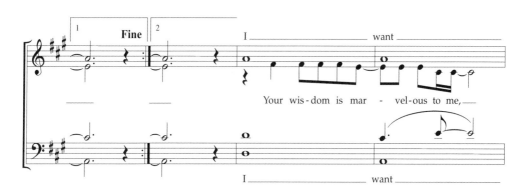
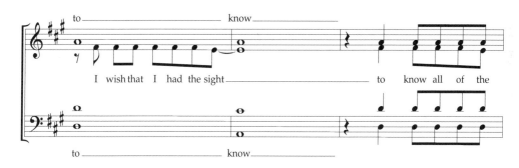

246   I Love Your Word

WORDS: David Eastman
MUSIC: David Eastman
Copyright © 2004 by David Eastman. Licensed from River City Music, LLC.

The Power

247

WORDS: Devon Sparks
MUSIC: Devon Sparks
Copyright © 2002 by Devon Sparks. Licensed from River City Music, LLC.

248 Lord I Want to Thank You

WORDS: Henry Lawson
MUSIC: Henry Lawson. Arr. by Jay Berckley
Copyright © 2007 by Henry Lawson and Jay Berckley. Licensed from River City Music, LLC.

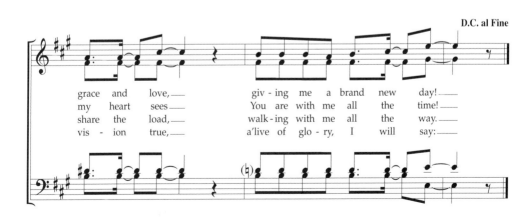

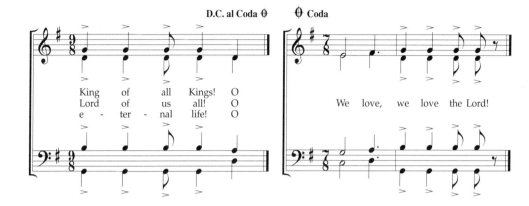

Mark 12:28-31
The Greatest Commandment

[28]One of the teachers of the law came and heard them debating. Noticing that Jesus had given them a good answer, he asked him, "Of all the commandments, which is the most important?"

[29]"The most important one," answered Jesus, "is this: 'Hear, O Israel: The Lord our God, the Lord is one. 30 Love the Lord your God with all your heart and with all your soul and with all your mind and with all your strength.' 31 The second is this: 'Love your neighbor as yourself.' There is no commandment greater than these."

250 Let's Worship

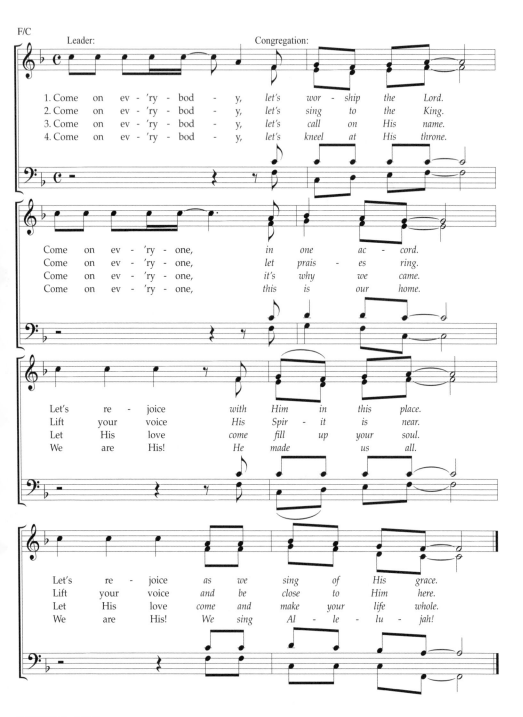

WORDS: Paul Chilson
MUSIC: Paul Chilson
Copyright © 2006 by Paul Chilson. Licensed from River City Music, LLC.

Mercy

251

WORDS: John Slate
MUSIC: John Slate
Copyright © 2006 by John Slate. Licensed from River City Music, LLC.

255 Let the Light Shine Down

1. Let the light shine down on me. Lift my eyes that I may see.
2. When the path I walk is dark, when the clouds are all I see,
3. When my faith is weak and small, when my fears are all I see,
4. When my sword is lift-ed high, when I bask in vic-to-ry,
5. When I live my fi-nal day, when my ship sails 'cross the sea,

Let the light shine down, on this way-ward ground,

Let the light shine down on me.

Finale: Sing last time (after all verses and chorus), slowing down and with dynamics

Let the light shine down on me.

WORDS: Geoff Fawcett
MUSIC: Geoff Fawcett
Copyright © 2002 by Geoff Fawcett. Licensed from River City Music, LLC.

My Soul Glorifies the Lord 256

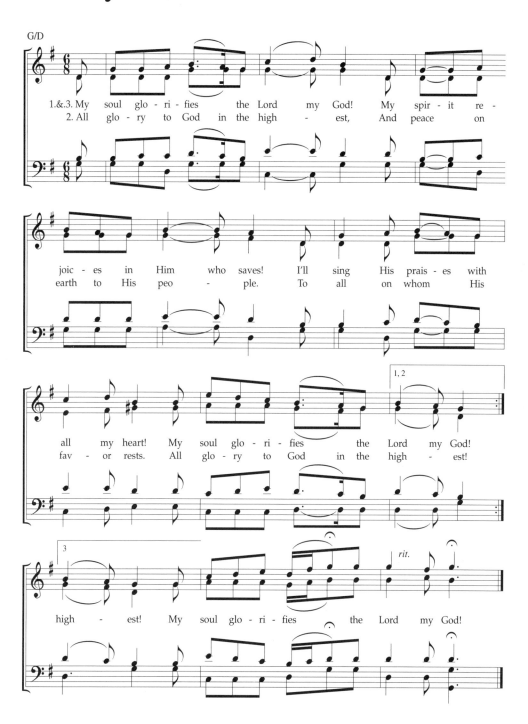

WORDS: Ivan Lyashenko and Maria Lyashenko
MUSIC: Ivan Lyashenko and Maria Lyashenko
Copyright © 2004 by Ivan Lyashenko and Maria Lyashenko. Licensed from River City Music, LLC.

257 My Heart Rejoices

WORDS: Ross Lippencott
MUSIC: Ross Lippencott
Copyright © 2011 by Ross Lippencott/NYCCOC. Licensed from River City Music, LLC.

258 # No Other Love

WORDS: J. Brian Craig
MUSIC: J. Brian Craig
Copyright © 2006 by J. Brian Craig. Licensed from River City Music, LLC.

Open My Eyes

260

1. How do we gauge the gap that stands be-tween the dark and light?
2. How does a sleep-ing heart with sim-ple words a-wak-en?
3. How can the sin-ful be a source for You of great de-light?

How can cor-rup-ted man and the Ho-ly Fa-ther re-u-nite?
Why did the per-fect Sav-ior love me though He was for-sak-en?
How can a low-ly man ap-proach a throne of heav-en's height?

How can the wick-ed be so loved?
How can the Ho-ly live with me?
How can the shame-ful be so loved?

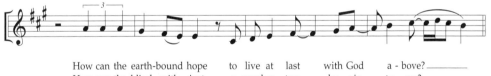

How can the earth-bound hope to live at last with God a-bove?
How can the blind with just a word or two be-gin to see?
How can the earth-bound hope to live at last with God a-bove?

Show me Your love, teach me Your grace.

WORDS: David Eastman
MUSIC: David Eastman
Copyright © 2005 by David Eastman. Licensed from River City Music, LLC.

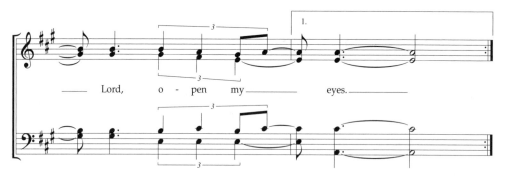

261 Only God

WORDS: J. Brian Craig
MUSIC: J. Brian Craig
Copyright © 2001 by J. Brian Craig. Licensed from River City Music, LLC.

262 Our God

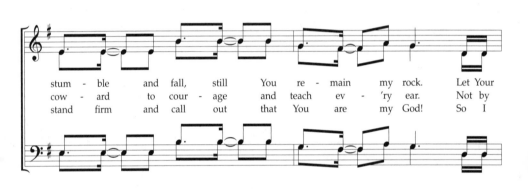
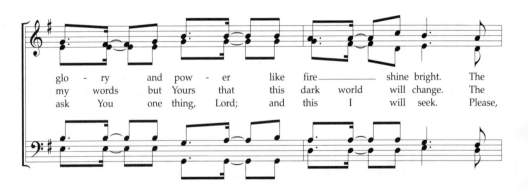

WORDS: Jacob Tacher
MUSIC: Jacob Tacher
Copyright © 2010 by Jacob Tacher. Licensed from River City Music, LLC.

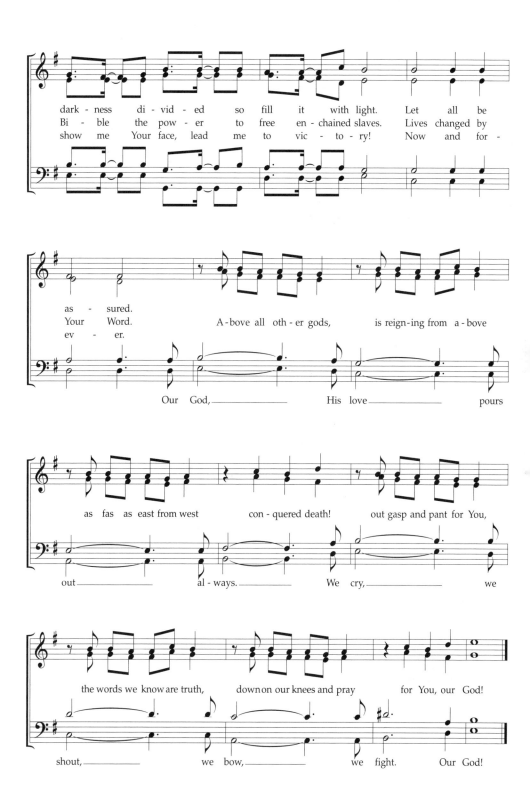

263 O Se

English translation from Yoruba:
Chorus: Thank You. Thank You so much. Thank You so much. Thank You, Father.
Verse: We have come to thank You, Our God. Almighty God, King, I worship You, my God. We thank You, Father.

WORDS: Chorus: traditional Nigerian song, Verses: Ayo Owodunni
MUSIC: Ayo Owodunni
Copyright © 2008 by Ayo Owodunni. Licensed from River City Music, LLC.

Praises Heard Around the World 264

WORDS: Tony Martin and J. Brian Craig
MUSIC: Tony Martin and J. Brian Craig
Copyright © 2007 by Tony Martin and J. Brian Craig. Licensed from River City Music, LLC.

265 O Rock of Ages

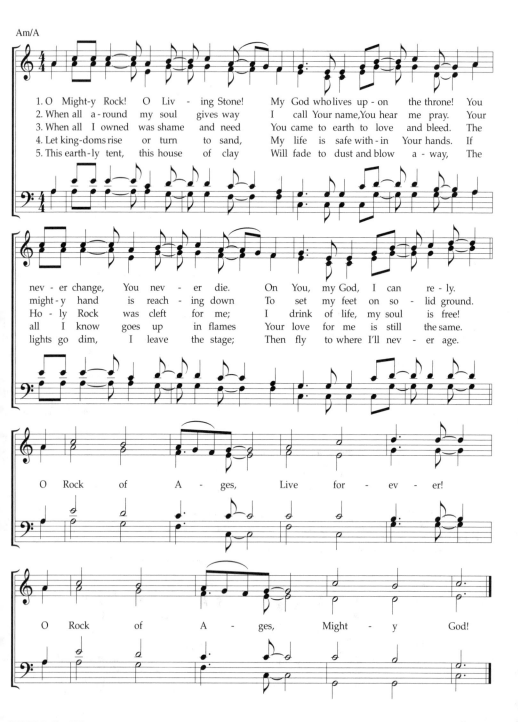

1. O Mighty Rock! O Living Stone! My God who lives upon the throne! You never change, You never die. On You, my God, I can rely.
2. When all around my soul gives way, I call Your name, You hear me pray. Your mighty hand is reaching down To set my feet on solid ground.
3. When all I owned was shame and need, You came to earth to love and bleed. The Holy Rock was cleft for me; I drink of life, my soul is free!
4. Let kingdoms rise or turn to sand, My life is safe within Your hands. If all I know goes up in flames Your love for me is still the same.
5. This earthly tent, this house of clay Will fade to dust and blow away, The lights go dim, I leave the stage; Then fly to where I'll never age.

O Rock of Ages, Live forever!
O Rock of Ages, Mighty God!

WORDS: Geoff Fawcett
MUSIC: Geoff Fawcett
Copyright © 2004 by Geoff Fawcett. Licensed from River City Music, LLC.

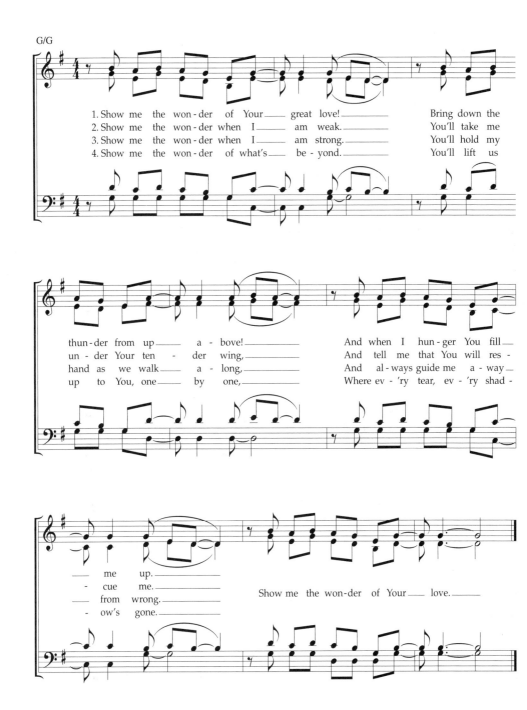# Show Me the Wonder 266

1. Show me the wonder of Your great love! Bring down the thunder from up above! And when I hunger You fill me up.
2. Show me the wonder when I am weak. You'll take me under Your tender wing, And tell me that You will rescue me.
3. Show me the wonder when I am strong. You'll hold my hand as we walk along, And always guide me away from wrong.
4. Show me the wonder of what's beyond. You'll lift us up to You, one by one, Where ev'ry tear, ev'ry shadow's gone.

Show me the wonder of Your love.

WORDS: J. Brian Craig
MUSIC: J. Brian Craig
Copyright © 2005 by J. Brian Craig. Licensed from River City Music, LLC.

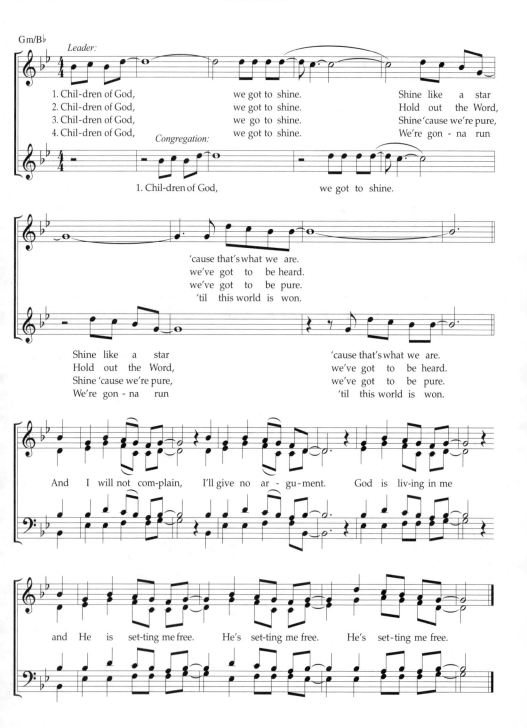

Sing and Rejoice

268

WORDS: Gerri Bernitt
MUSIC: Gerri Bernitt
Copyright © 2007 by Gerri Bernitt. Licensed from River City Music, LLC.

269 Set Apart

WORDS: J. Brian Craig
MUSIC: J. Brian Craig
Copyright © 2006 by J. Brian Craig. Licensed from River City Music, LLC.

270 Shake the Earth

WORDS: Nilson Ramirez
MUSIC: S. Chase Mackintosh
Copyright © 2010 by Nilson Ramirez and S. Chase Mackintosh. Licensed from River City Music, LLC.

Sing My Way Home 271

WORDS: Danny Figgins
MUSIC: Danny Figgins
Copyright © 2008 by Danny Figgins. Licensed from River City Music, LLC.

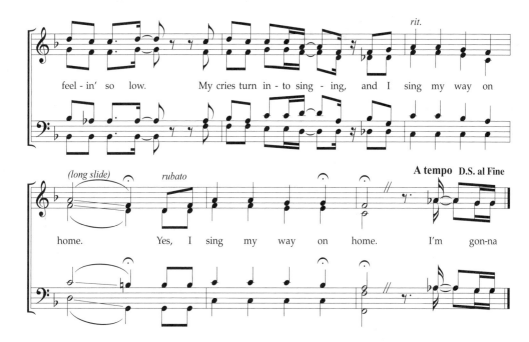

Sing of His Righteousness 272

WORDS: Barish Golland
MUSIC: Barish Golland
Copyright © 2005 by Barish Golland. Licensed from River City Music, LLC.

273 The Spirit's Fire

WORDS: J. Brian Craig
MUSIC: J. Brian Craig
Copyright © 2003 by J. Brian Craig. Licensed from River City Music, LLC.

We Make It Our Goal to Please Him 274

WORDS: J. Brian Craig. Based on 2 Corinthians 5:1-11.
MUSIC: J. Brian Craig.
Copyright © 2008 by J. Brian Craig.. Licensed from River City Music, LLC.

275 Song of Moses

1. Now Pharaoh and his army they were thrown into the sea, while Moses and the people they were given victory. Let's praise the Lord, praise His holy name. You know my God, He is a warrior and the Lord is His name. My God, He is a warrior and the Lord is His name.

2. The Lord, He is my strength; I know the Lord, He is my song. The Lord is my salvation when my enemies are strong. Let's praise the Lord...

3. In Your unfailing love, You'll lead the people You've redeemed; and with Your strength You'll guide us, You will bring to life our dreams. Let's praise the Lord...

WORDS: John Slate. Based on Exodus 15.
MUSIC: John Slate.
Copyright © 2006 by John Slate. Licensed from River City Music, LLC.

276 Stand Defiant

WORDS: Nilson Ramirez
MUSIC: S. Chase Mackintosh
Copyright © 2010 by Nilson Ramirez and S. Chase Mackintosh. Licensed from River City Music, LLC.

277 Strong in the Grace

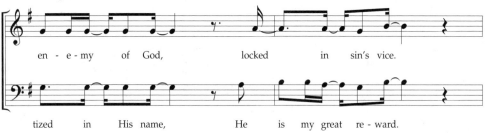

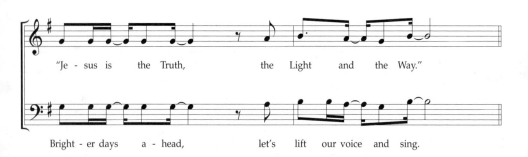

WORDS: Tony Martin
MUSIC: Tony Martin
Copyright © 2010 by Tony Martin. Licensed from River City Music, LLC.

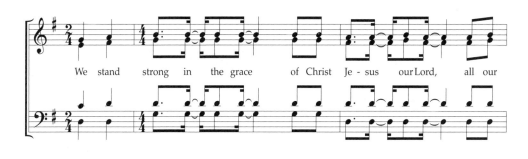

278 Strong in Spirit

WORDS: Mark Haven Hoyle. Based on Luke 1:80.
MUSIC: Mark Haven Hoyle
Copyright © 2006 by Mark Haven Hoyle. Licensed from River City Music, LLC.

In the de-sert I be-came strong in spir-it.

Luke 1:67-80
Zechariah's Song

⁶⁷Zechariah [the father of John] was filled with the
>   Holy Spirit and prophesied:
⁶⁸"Praise be to the Lord, the God of Israel,
>   because he has come to his people and redeemed them.
⁶⁹He has raised up a horn of salvation for us
>   in the house of his servant David
⁷⁰(as he said through his holy prophets of long ago),
⁷¹salvation from our enemies
>   and from the hand of all who hate us—
⁷²to show mercy to our ancestors
>   and to remember his holy covenant,
⁷³the oath he swore to our father Abraham:
⁷⁴to rescue us from the hand of our enemies,
>   and to enable us to serve him without fear
⁷⁵in holiness and righteousness before him all our days.

⁷⁶And you, my child, will be called a prophet of the Most
>   High;
for you will go on before the Lord to prepare the way for
>   him,
⁷⁷to give his people the knowledge of salvation
>   through the forgiveness of their sins,
⁷⁸because of the tender mercy of our God,
>   by which the rising sun will come to us from heaven
⁷⁹to shine on those living in darkness
>   and in the shadow of death,
to guide our feet into the path of peace."
>   ⁸⁰And the child grew and became strong in spirit;
and he lived in the desert until he appeared publicly to Israel.

White As Snow

1. I was stumbling in the darkness, lost without a home.
2. Blood that flowed down from the cross, it stained the earth below,
3. Spirit gives me comfort and He shows the way to go;
4. You stoop down and make me great; My cup, it overflows.

You took sins that were as scarlet, made them white as snow.
Red with love that paid the price to make me white as snow.
Now He lives inside me, 'cause You made me white as snow.
Full of all You've blessed me with, You make me white as snow.

Turn my dark into light and You make me white as snow!
Out of death, into life and You make me white as snow!

WORDS: J. Brian Craig
MUSIC: J. Brian Craig and Tony Martin
Copyright © 2006 by J. Brian Craig and Tony Martin. Licensed from River City Music, LLC.

Unshakable Faith 280

WORDS: Ross Lippencott
MUSIC: Ross Lippencott
Copyright © 2010 by Ross Lippencott. Licensed from River City Music, LLC.

Matthew 7:24-27
The Wise and Foolish Builders

²⁴"Therefore everyone who hears these words of mine and puts them into practice is like a wise man who built his house on the rock. ²⁵The rain came down, the streams rose, and the winds blew and beat against that house; yet it did not fall, because it had its foundation on the rock. ²⁶But everyone who hears these words of mine and does not put them into practice is like a foolish man who built his house on sand. ²⁷The rain came down, the streams rose, and the winds blew and beat against that house, and it fell with a great crash."

The Goodness of the Lord 282

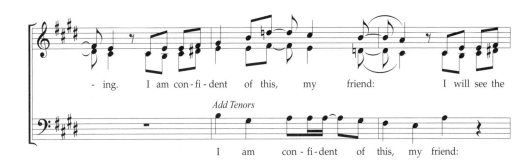

WORDS: Todd Gilmore
MUSIC: Todd Gilmore
Copyright © 2005 by Todd Gilmore. Licensed from River City Music, LLC.

1st time repeat: Go to BRIDGE, sing Bridge v2, then Verse 3, then from [A] to end slowly.

Isaiah 55:8-9

[8]"For my thoughts are not your thoughts,
neither are your ways my ways,"
declares the LORD.

[9]"As the heavens are higher than the earth,
so are my ways higher than your ways
and my thoughts than your thoughts."

284 Surrendered

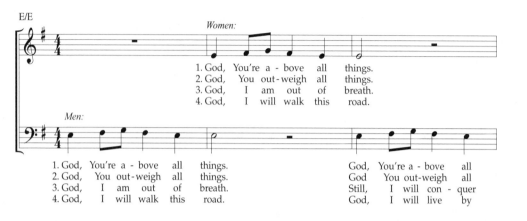
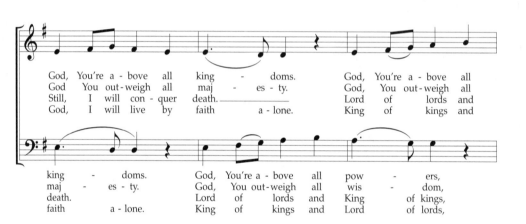
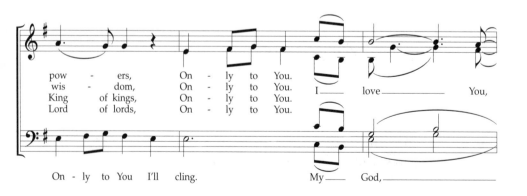

WORDS: Nilson Ramirez
MUSIC: S. Chase Mackintosh
Copyright © 2010 by Nilson Ramirez and S. Chase Mackintosh. Licensed from River City Music, LLC.

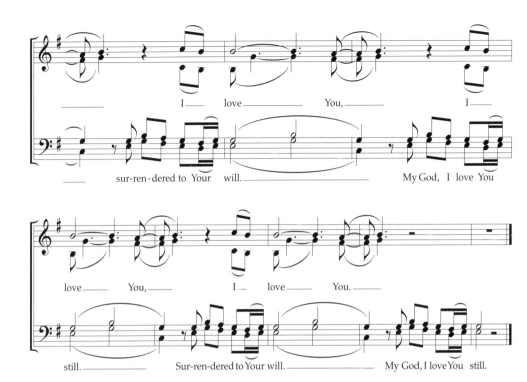

Matthew 26:36-42
Gethsemane

³⁶Then Jesus went with his disciples to a place called Gethsemane, and he said to them, "Sit here while I go over there and pray." ³⁷He took Peter and the two sons of Zebedee along with him, and he began to be sorrowful and troubled. ³⁸Then he said to them, "My soul is overwhelmed with sorrow to the point of death. Stay here and keep watch with me."

³⁹Going a little farther, he fell with his face to the ground and prayed, "My Father, if it is possible, may this cup be taken from me. Yet not as I will, but as you will."

⁴⁰Then he returned to his disciples and found them sleeping. "Couldn't you men keep watch with me for one hour?" he asked Peter. ⁴¹"Watch and pray so that you will not fall into temptation. The spirit is willing, but the flesh is weak."

⁴²He went away a second time and prayed, "My Father, if it is not possible for this cup to be taken away unless I drink it, may your will be done."

285 Your Name

WORDS: David Eastman
MUSIC: David Eastman
Copyright © 2005 by David Eastman. Licensed from River City Music, LLC.

286 Surefooted

1. Well, I am sure-foot-ed as a deer on the moun-tain heights.
2. Well, I am sure thank-ful for the life I have found in Christ.
3. Well, I am sure grate-ful I have friends walk-ing in the light.
4. Well, I am sure hap-py there's a home where I'll nev-er die.

I can run, not grow wea-ry; can walk, not grow faint.
My God will res-cue me when Sa-tan's in chase. I'm sure-
faint. And like a deer,

WORDS: Mark Haven Hoyle. Based on 2 Samuel 22:34.
MUSIC: Mark Haven Hoyle.
Copyright © 2005 by Mark Haven Hoyle. Licensed from River City Music, LLC.

2 Samuel 22:29-37

[29] You, Lord, are my lamp;
   the Lord turns my darkness into light.
[30] With your help I can advance against a troop;
   with my God I can scale a wall.
[31] "As for God, his way is perfect:
   The Lord's word is flawless;
   he shields all who take refuge in him.
[32] For who is God besides the Lord?
   And who is the Rock except our God?
[33] It is God who arms me with strength
   and keeps my way secure.
[34] He makes my feet like the feet of a deer;
   he causes me to stand on the heights.
[35] He trains my hands for battle;
   my arms can bend a bow of bronze.
[36] You give me your shield of victory;
   you stoop down to make me great.
[37] You broaden the path beneath me,
   so that my ankles do not turn.

Traditional Hymns

There's Power in the Blood 350

1. Would you be free from your burden of sin? There's pow'r in the blood, pow'r in the blood; Would you o'er evil a victory win? There's wonderful pow'r in the blood.
2. Would you be free from your passion and pride? There's pow'r in the blood, pow'r in the blood; Come for a cleansing to Calvary's tide; There's wonderful pow'r in the blood.
3. Would you be whiter, much whiter than snow? There's pow'r in the blood, pow'r in the blood; Sin-stains are lost in its life-giving flow; There's wonderful pow'r in the blood.
4. Would you do service for Jesus your king? There's pow'r in the blood, pow'r in the blood; Would you live daily His praises to sing? There's wonderful pow'r in the blood.

There is pow'r, pow'r, wonder-working pow'r in the blood of the Lamb; There is pow'r, pow'r, wonder-working pow'r in the precious blood of the Lamb.

WORDS: Lewis Jones, 1899
MUSIC: Lewis Jones, 1899

Glorious Things of Thee Are Spoken 352

1. Glorious things of Thee are spoken, Zion, city of our God! He whose word cannot be broken formed thee for His own abode: On the Rock of ages founded, What can shake thy sure repose? With salvation's walls surrounded Thou may'st smile at all thy foes.

2. See, the streams of living waters, springing from eternal love, Well supply thy sons and daughters, and all fear of want remove: Who can faint while such a river ever flows their thirst t'assuage? Grace, which, like the Lord the giver, Never fails from age to age.

3. Savior, since of Zion's city I, through grace a member am, Let the world deride or pity, I will glory in Thy name. Fading is the worldling's pleasure, All his boasted pomp and show; Solid joys and lasting treasure, None but Zion's children know.

WORDS: John Newton, 1779
MUSIC: Franz Joseph Haydn, 1797

(To "assuage" is to satisfy.)

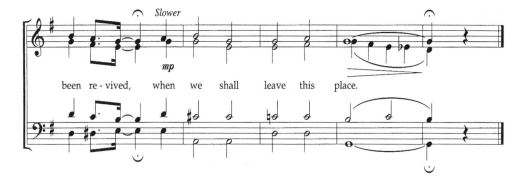

Take My Life, and Let It Be 354

1. Take my life, and let it be Con-se-cra-ted, Lord, to Thee;
2. Take my hands, and let them move At the im-pulse of Thy love;
3. Take my voice, and let me sing Al-ways, on-ly, for my King;
4. Take my sil-ver and my gold: Not a mite would I with-hold;
5. Take my will, and make it Thine: It shall be no long-er mine;
6. Take my love, my Lord, I pour At Thy feet its trea-sure store;

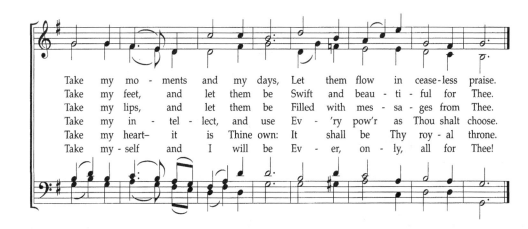

Take my mo-ments and my days, Let them flow in cease-less praise.
Take my feet, and let them be Swift and beau-ti-ful for Thee.
Take my lips, and let them be Filled with mes-sa-ges from Thee.
Take my in-tel-lect, and use Ev-'ry pow'r as Thou shalt choose.
Take my heart— it is Thine own: It shall be Thy roy-al throne.
Take my-self and I will be Ev-er, on-ly, all for Thee!

WORDS: Frances R. Havergal, 1874
MUSIC: Mozart, 1821

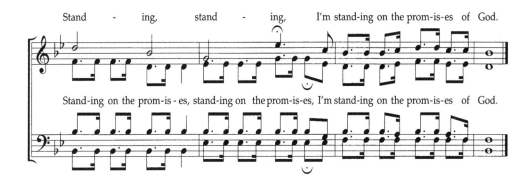

Where Could I Go? 356

1. Liv-ing be-low in this old sin-ful world, Hard-ly a com-fort can af-ford;
2. Neigh-bors are kind, I love them ev-'ry one, We get a-long in sweet ac-cord;
3. Life here is grand with friends I love so dear, Com-fort I get from God's own word;

CHORUS: Where could I go, O where could I go, Seek-ing a ref-uge for my soul?

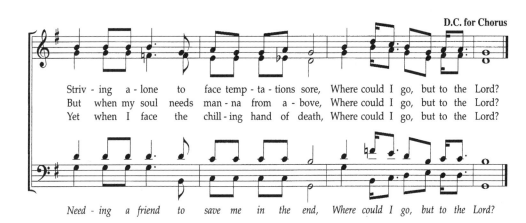

Striv-ing a-lone to face temp-ta-tions sore, Where could I go, but to the Lord?
But when my soul needs man-na from a-bove, Where could I go, but to the Lord?
Yet when I face the chill-ing hand of death, Where could I go, but to the Lord?

Need-ing a friend to save me in the end, Where could I go, but to the Lord?

WORDS: J. B. Coats, 1940
MUSIC: J. B. Coats, 1940
© 1940 Stamps-Baxter Music (BMI) (admin. by Brentwood-Benson Music Publishing, Inc., 365 Great Circle Rd., Nashville, TN 37228). All rights reserved. Used by permission.

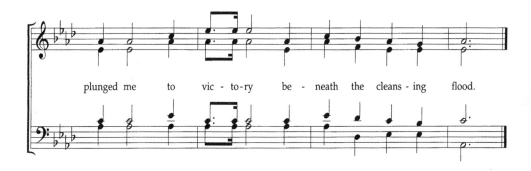

358 The Old Rugged Cross

1. On a hill far away stood an old rugged cross, the emblem of suff'ring and shame; And I love that old cross where the dearest and best, for a world of lost sinners was slain.
2. O that old rugged cross, so despised by the world, has a wondrous attraction for me; For the dear Lamb of God left His glory above, to bear it to dark Calvary.
3. In that old rugged cross, stained with blood so divine, a wondrous beauty I see; For 'twas on that old cross Jesus suffered and died, to pardon and sanctify me.
4. To the old rugged cross I will ever be true, its shame and reproach gladly bear; Then He'll call me some day, to my home far away, where His glory forever I'll share.

So I'll cherish the old rugged cross, till my trophies at last I lay down,
So I'll cherish the cross, the old rugged cross, till my trophies at last I lay down,

WORDS: George Bennard, 1913
MUSIC: George Bennard, 1913

360 A Mighty Fortress

Slow and majestic

1. A mighty fortress is our God, A bulwark never failing; Our helper, He, amid the flood Of mortal ills prevailing; For still our ancient foe Doth seek to work us woe; His craft and pow'r are great, And, armed with cruel hate, On earth is not his equal.

2. Did we in our own strength confide, Our striving would be losing; Were not the right man on our side, The man of God's own choosing: Dost ask who that may be? Christ Jesus, it is He! Lord Sabaoth His name, From age to age the same, And He must win the battle.

3. And tho' this world, with demons filled, Should threaten to undo us, We will not fear, for God hath willed His truth to triumph through us: Let goods and kindred go, This mortal life also; The body they may kill: God's truth abideth still, His kingdom is forever.

WORDS: Martin Luther, 1529; trans. Frederick M. Hedge
MUSIC: Martin Luther, 1529

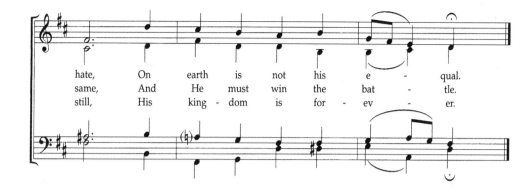

God Moves in a Mysterious Way 361

WORDS: William Cowper, 1774
MUSIC: Scottish Psalter (Hart's Psalms of David, 1615; Thomas Ravenscroft, 1621)

362 For Those Tears, I Died

WORDS: Marsha J. Stevens, 1969
MUSIC: Marsha J. Stevens, 1969

© 1969 Bud John Songs, Inc. (ASCAP) (admin. by EMI Christian Music Publishing, 101 Winners Circle, Brentwood, TN 37024). All rights reserved. Used by permission.

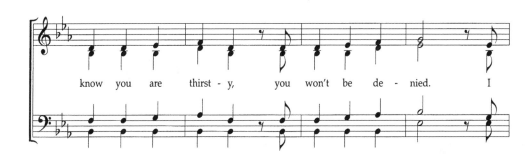

Precious Lord 364

WORDS: Thomas Dorsey, 1938
MUSIC: Thomas Dorsey, 1938
© 1938 Unichappell Music, Inc. Copyright renewed. International copyright secured. All rights reserved.
Used by permission.

365 When the Roll Is Called

WORDS: J. M. Black, 1893
MUSIC: J. M. Black, 1893

Glory Be to Jesus 366

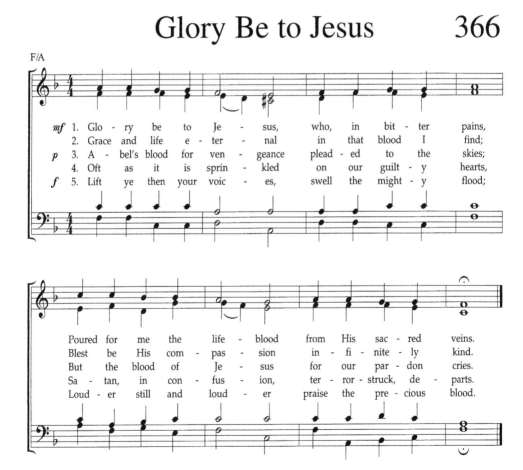

1. Glory be to Jesus, who, in bitter pains, Poured for me the lifeblood from His sacred veins.
2. Grace and life eternal in that blood I find; Blest be His compassion infinitely kind.
3. Abel's blood for vengeance pleaded to the skies; But the blood of Jesus for our pardon cries.
4. Oft as it is sprinkled on our guilty hearts, Satan, in confusion, terror-struck, departs.
5. Lift ye then your voices, swell the mighty flood; Louder still and louder praise the precious blood.

WORDS: Italian hymn; trans. Edward Caswell, 1854
MUSIC: Friedrich Filits; 1876

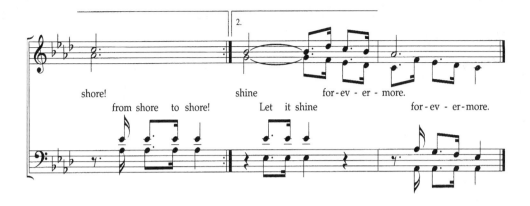

How Sweet, How Heavenly 370

1. How sweet, how heav'n-ly, is the sight, when those that love the Lord, In one an-oth-er's peace de-light, and so ful-fill the Word.
2. When each can feel his bro-ther's sigh, and with him bear a part; When sor-row flows from eye to eye, and joy from heart to heart.
3. When, free from en-vy, scorn and pride, our wish-es all a-bove, Each can his bro-ther's fail-ings hide, and show a bro-ther's love.
4. When love in one de-light-ful stream through ev-'ry bo-som flows, When un-ion sweet and dear es-teem in ev-'ry ac-tion glows.
5. Love is the gold-en chain that binds the hap-py souls a-bove; And he's an heir of heav'n who finds his bo-som glows with love.

WORDS: Joseph Swain, 1792
MUSIC: William B. Bradbury, 1844

371 My Jesus, I Love Thee

F/F

1. My Jesus, I love Thee, I know Thou art mine;
2. I love Thee, be-cause Thou hast first lov-ed me,
3. In man-sions of glo-ry and end-less de-light,

For Thee all the fol-lies of sin I re-sign;
And pur-chased my par-don on Cal-va-ry's tree;
I'll ev-er a-dore Thee in heav-en so bright;

My gra-cious Re-deem-er, my Sav-ior art Thou;
I love Thee for wear-ing the thorns on Thy brow;
I'll sing with the glit-ter-ing crown on my brow;

If ev-er I loved Thee, my Je-sus, 'tis now.

WORDS: William K. Featherstone, 1876
MUSIC: Adoniram J. Gordon, 1876

Shall We Gather at the River?

1. Shall we gather at the river, Where bright angel feet have trod,
2. On the margin of the river, Washing up its silver spray,
3. Ere we reach the shining river, Lay we ev-'ry burden down;
4. At the smiling of the river, Mirror of the Savior's face,

With its crystal tide forever Flowing by the throne of God? Oh,
We will walk and worship ever, All the happy, golden day. Oh,
Grace our spirits will deliver, And provide a robe and crown. Oh,
Saints whom death will never sever Lift their songs of saving grace. Oh,

yes, we'll gather at the river, The beautiful, the beautiful river,
beautiful, the river,

To Optional Ending (Use opt. ending on last chorus if desired)

Gather with the saints at the river, That flows by the throne of God. God.

WORDS: Robert Lowry, 1864
MUSIC: Robert Lowry, 1864; arr. E. Sherwin Mackintosh, 1992

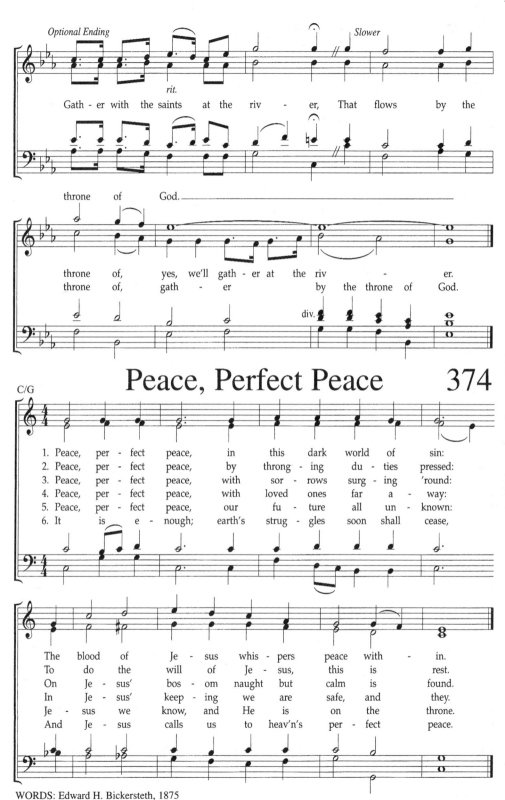

I Know That My Redeemer Lives 376

1. I know that my Redeemer lives, And ever prays for me;
A token of His love He gives, a pledge of liberty.
2. I find Him lifting up my head; He brings salvation near;
His presence makes me free indeed, and He will soon appear.
3. He wills that I should holy be: Can I withstand His will?
The counsel of His grace in me, He surely shall fulfill.
4. Jesus, I hang upon Thy word, I steadfastly believe
Thou wilt return and claim me, Lord, and to Thyself receive.

WORDS: Charles Wesley, 1742 (based on Job 19:25)
MUSIC: George Frederick Handel, 1741 (from "The Messiah")

377 Ten Thousand Angels

1. They bound the hands of Jesus in the garden where He prayed; They led Him through the streets in shame. They spat upon the Savior, so pure and free from sin; They said: "Crucify Him; He's to blame."
2. Upon His precious head they placed a crown of thorns; They laughed and said: "Behold the King." They struck Him and they cursed Him and mocked His holy name— All alone He suffered ev-'ry-thing.
3. To the howling mob He yielded; He did not for mercy cry. The cross of shame He took alone. And when He cried: "It's finished," He gave Himself to die; Salvation's wondrous plan was done.

He could have called ten thousand angels to destroy the world

WORDS: Ray Overholt, 1959
MUSIC: Ray Overholt, 1959
(the world)

© 1959 Lillenas Publishing Co. (admin. by The Copyright Company, 40 Music Sq. E, Nashville, TN 37203). All rights reserved. International copyright secured. Used by permission.

379 Praise Him! Praise Him!

1. Praise Him! Praise Him! Jesus, our blessed Redeemer! Sing, O earth, His wonderful love proclaim! Hail Him, hail Him, highest angels in glory! Strength and honor give to His holy name! Like a shepherd, Jesus will guard His children; In His arms He
2. Praise Him! Praise Him! Jesus, our blessed Redeemer! For our sins He suffered, and bled, and died; He, our Rock, our hope of eternal salvation; Hail Him, hail Him, Jesus the crucified! Sound His praises! Jesus, who bore our sorrows, Love unbounded,
3. Praise Him! Praise Him! Jesus, our blessed Redeemer! Heav'nly portals loud with hosannas ring! Jesus, Savior, reigneth forever and ever; Crown Him, crown Him Prophet, and Priest, and King! Christ is coming, over the world victorious, Pow'r and glory

WORDS: Fanny J. Crosby, 1869
MUSIC: Chester G. Allen, 1869

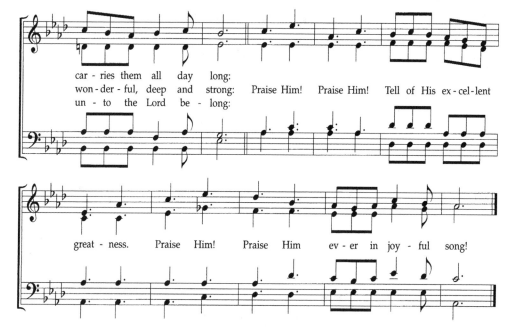

What Can Wash Away My Sin? 380

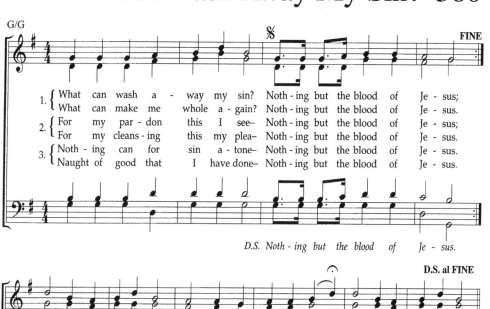

1. What can wash away my sin? Nothing but the blood of Jesus;
   What can make me whole again? Nothing but the blood of Jesus.
2. For my pardon this I see— Nothing but the blood of Jesus;
   For my cleansing this my plea— Nothing but the blood of Jesus.
3. Nothing can for sin atone— Nothing but the blood of Jesus.
   Naught of good that I have done— Nothing but the blood of Jesus.

D.S. Nothing but the blood of Jesus.

Oh, precious is the flow That makes me white as snow; No other fount I know,

WORDS: Robert Lowry, 1876 (based on Revelation 7:14)
MUSIC: Robert Lowry, 1876

381 There Is Much to Do

E♭/G

1. There is much to do, there's work on ev-'ry hand, Hark! the cry for
2. There's the plain-tive cry of mourn-ing souls dis-tressed, And the sigh of
3. There are hun-g'ring souls who cry a-loud for bread, With the bread of
4. There are souls who lin-ger on the brink of woe, Lord, I must not,

help comes ring-ing through the land; Je-sus calls for reap-ers,
hearts who seek but find no rest; These should have my love and
life they're long-ing to be fed; Shall they starve and fam-ish
can not, bear to let them go; Let me go and tell them:

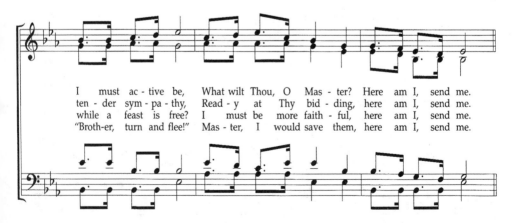

I must ac-tive be, What wilt Thou, O Mas-ter? Here am I, send me.
ten-der sym-pa-thy, Read-y at Thy bid-ding, here am I, send me.
while a feast is free? I must be more faith-ful, here am I, send me.
"Broth-er, turn and flee!" Mas-ter, I would save them, here am I, send me.

WORDS: M. W. Spencer
MUSIC: M. W. Spencer

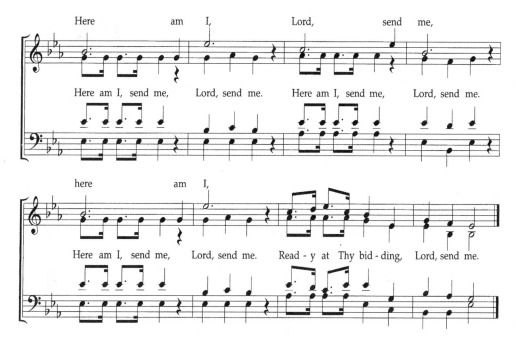

When I Survey the Wondrous Cross 382

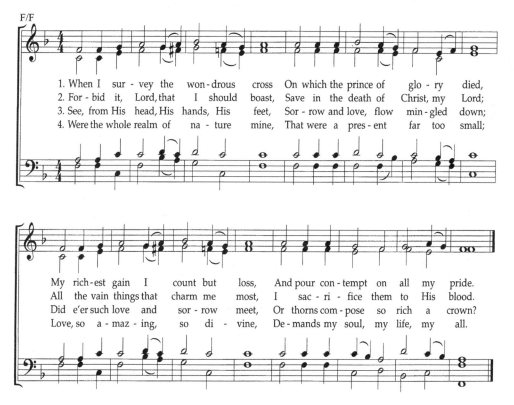

1. When I survey the wondrous cross On which the prince of glory died, My richest gain I count but loss, And pour contempt on all my pride.
2. Forbid it, Lord, that I should boast, Save in the death of Christ, my Lord; All the vain things that charm me most, I sacrifice them to His blood.
3. See, from His head, His hands, His feet, Sorrow and love, flow mingled down; Did e'er such love and sorrow meet, Or thorns compose so rich a crown?
4. Were the whole realm of nature mine, That were a present far too small; Love, so amazing, so divine, Demands my soul, my life, my all.

WORDS: Isaac Watts, 1707
MUSIC: Gregorian chant; arr. Lowell Mason, 1824

Rise Up, O Men of God   384

1. Rise up, O men of God! Have done with less-er things; Give heart and mind and soul and strength to serve the King of kings.
2. Rise up, O men of God! His King-dom tar-ries long; Bring in the day of broth-er-hood and end the night of wrong.
3. Rise up, O men of God! The church for you doth wait, Her strength un-e-qual to her task; Rise up, and make her great!
4. Lift high the cross of Christ! Tread where His feet have trod; As broth-ers of the Son of Man, *Rise up, O men of God!

WORDS: William P. Merrill, 1911
MUSIC: William Walter, 1894
Used by permission of the Presbyterian Outlook, Richmond, Va.

*Repeat final phrase of final verse

Make Me a Channel of Your Peace 388

1. Make me a chan-nel of Your peace. Where there is ha-tred,
2. Make me a chan-nel of Your peace. Where there's de-spair in

let me bring Your love. Where there is in-ju-ry, Your par-don,
life, let me bring hope. Where there is dark-ness, Let me bring

Lord, And where there's doubt, true faith in You.
light, And where there's sad-ness, ev-er joy.

WORDS: Traditional
MUSIC: Traditional

389 We'll Work till Jesus Comes

1. O land of rest, for thee I sigh! When will the moment come, When I shall lay my armor by, And dwell in peace at home?
2. To Jesus Christ I fled for rest; He bade me cease to roam, And lean for succor on His breast Till He conduct me home.
3. I sought at once my Savior's side: No more my steps shall roam, With Him I'll brave death's chilling tide, And reach my heav'nly home.

Refrain: We'll work till Jesus comes, We'll work till Jesus comes, We'll work till Jesus comes, And we'll be gathered home.

WORDS: Elizabeth Mills, 1836
MUSIC: William Miller, 1859

What a Friend We Have in Jesus 390

1. What a friend we have in Jesus, All our sins and griefs to bear!
What a privilege to carry Ev-'rything to God in prayer!
Oh, what peace we often forfeit, Oh, what needless pain we bear,
All because we do not carry Ev-'rything to God in prayer.

2. Have we trials and temptations? Is there trouble anywhere?
We should never be discouraged: Take it to the Lord in prayer;
Can we find a friend so faithful, Who will all our sorrows share?
Jesus knows our ev-'ry weakness; Take it to the Lord in prayer.

3. Are we weak and heavy-laden, Cumbered with a load of care?
Precious Savior, still our refuge; Take it to the Lord in prayer;
Do thy friends despise, forsake thee? Take it to the Lord in prayer;
In His arms He'll take and shield thee; Thou wilt find a solace there.

WORDS: Joseph M. Scriven, 1855
MUSIC: Charles C. Converse, 1868

391 This Is My Father's World

WORDS: Maltbie D. Babcock, 1901
MUSIC: Franklin L. Sheppard, 1915

To Canaan's Land I'm on My Way 392

1. To Canaan's land I'm on my way— Where the soul (of man) never dies;
2. A rose is blooming there for me— Where the soul (of man) never dies;
3. A love-light beams across the foam— Where the soul (of man) never dies;
4. I'm on my way to that fair land— Where the soul (of man) never dies;

My darkest night will turn to day— Where the soul (of man) never dies.
And I will spend eternity— Where the soul (of man) never dies.
It shines to light the shores of home— Where the soul (of man) never dies.
Where there will be no parting hand— Where the soul (of man) never dies.

No sad farewells, No tear-dimmed eyes,
Dear friends, there'll be no sad farewells, There'll be no tear-dimmed eyes,
Where all is love, And the soul never dies.
Where all is peace and joy and love, And the soul of man never dies.

WORDS: William M. Golden, 1914
MUSIC: William M. Golden, 1914

The Spacious Firmament on High 394

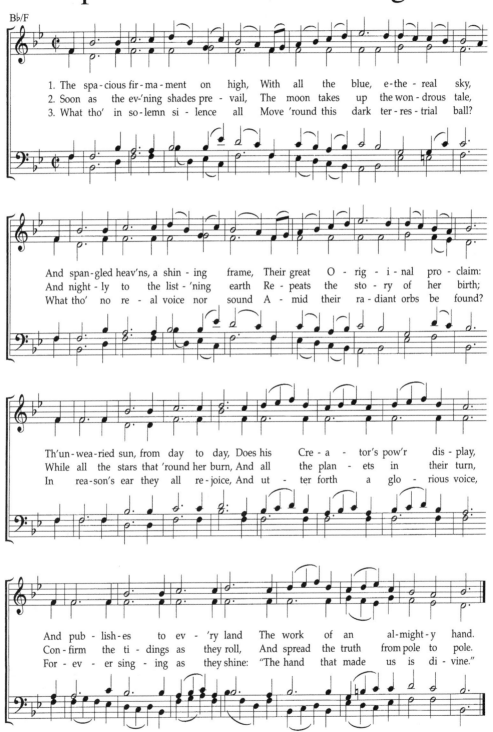

1. The spa-cious fir-ma-ment on high, With all the blue, e-the-real sky, And span-gled heav'ns, a shin-ing frame, Their great O-rig-i-nal pro-claim: Th'un-wea-ried sun, from day to day, Does his Cre-a-tor's pow'r dis-play, And pub-lish-es to ev-'ry land The work of an al-might-y hand.

2. Soon as the ev'ning shades pre-vail, The moon takes up the won-drous tale, And night-ly to the list-'ning earth Re-peats the sto-ry of her birth; While all the stars that 'round her burn, And all the plan-ets in their turn, Con-firm the ti-dings as they roll, And spread the truth from pole to pole.

3. What tho' in so-lemn si-lence all Move 'round this dark ter-res-trial ball? What tho' no re-al voice nor sound A-mid their ra-diant orbs be found? In rea-son's ear they all re-joice, And ut-ter forth a glo-rious voice, For-ev-er sing-ing as they shine: "The hand that made us is di-vine."

WORDS: John Addison, 1812 (based on Psalm 19)
MUSIC: Franz Joseph Haydn, 1798

395 Holy Father

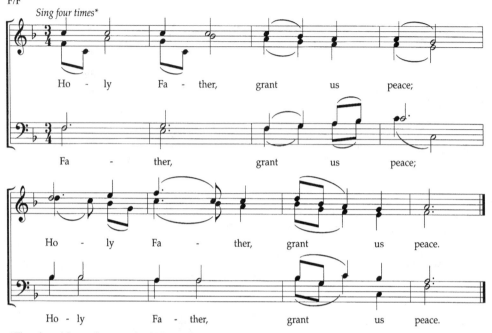

*First time: Altos only; second: add Sopranos; third: add Basses; fourth: add Tenors
WORDS: Traditional
MUSIC: Traditional

396 The Lord Bless You and Keep You

WORDS: Peter C. Lutkin, 1900 (based on Numbers 6:24-26)
MUSIC: Peter C. Lutkin, 1900

399 The Glory-Land Way

1. I'm in the way, the bright and shining way, I'm in the glory-land way; Telling the world that Jesus saves today, Yes, I'm in the glory-land way. (glory-land way;) I'm in the glory-land way; (glory-land way;) I'm in the glory-land way. (glory-land way.) Heaven is nearer and the way groweth clearer, For I'm in the glory-land way. (glory-land way.)

2. List to the call, the gospel call today, Get in the glory-land way. Wand'rers come home, O hasten to obey, For I'm in the glory-land way.

3. Onward I go, rejoicing in His love, I'm in the glory-land way. Soon I shall see Him in that home above, Oh, I'm in the glory-land way.

WORDS: James S. Torbett, 1924
MUSIC: James S. Torbett, 1924

Stand Up, Stand Up for Jesus 400

1. Stand up, stand up for Jesus! Ye soldiers of the cross; Lift high His royal banner, It must not suffer loss. From vict'ry unto vict'ry His army shall He lead, Till ev'ry foe is vanquished, And Christ is Lord indeed.

2. Stand up, stand up for Jesus! The trumpet call obey; Forth to the mighty conflict In this, His glorious day. Ye that are men now serve Him Against unnumbered foes; Let courage rise with danger, And strength to strength oppose.

3. Stand up, stand up for Jesus! Stand in His strength alone; The arm of flesh will fail you, Ye dare not trust your own. Put on the gospel armor, And watching unto prayer, Where duty calls, or danger, Be never wanting there.

4. Stand up, stand up for Jesus! The strife will not be long; This day the noise of battle, The next the victor's song. To him that overcometh A crown of life shall be; He with the King of Glory Shall reign eternally.

WORDS: George Duffeld, 1858
MUSIC: George J. Webb, 1837

401 Redeemed

WORDS: James Rowe, 1916
MUSIC: S. A. Ganus, 1916

Spirit of the Living God 402

WORDS: Daniel Iverson, 1935
MUSIC: Daniel Iverson, 1935
© 1935 Birdwing Music (ASCAP) (admin. by EMI Christian Music Publishing, 101 Winners Circle, Brentwood, TN 37024). All rights reserved. Used by permission.

403 Ring Out the Message

1. There's a message true and glad for the sinful and the sad,
Ring it out, ring it out;
It will give them courage new, it will help them to be true;
Ring it out, ring it out.

2. Tell the world of saving grace, make it known in ev-'ry place,
Ring it out, ring it out;
Help the needy ones to know Him from whom all blessings flow;
Ring it out, ring it out.

3. Sin and doubt to sweep away, till shall dawn the better day,
Ring it out, ring it out;
Till the sinful world be won for Jehovah's mighty Son;
Ring it out, ring it out.

Merrily ring, speed it away, message divine,
Ring out the word o'er land and

WORDS: James Rowe, 1911
MUSIC: Samuel W. Beasley, 1911

404 Nearer, Still Nearer

1. Nearer, still nearer, close to Thy heart,
Draw me my Savior, so precious Thou art;
Fold me, O fold me, close to Thy breast,
Shelter me safe in that haven of rest,

2. Nearer, still nearer, nothing I bring,
Naught as an off'ring to Jesus my King,
Only my sinful, now contrite heart;
Grant me the cleansing Thy blood doth impart,

3. Nearer, still nearer, Lord, to be Thine;
Sin, with its follies, I gladly resign,
All of its pleasures, pomp and its pride;
Give me but Jesus, my Lord crucified,

4. Nearer, still nearer, while life shall last,
Till, safe in glory my anchor is cast;
Through endless ages, ever to be;
Nearer, my Savior, still nearer to Thee,

WORDS: Leila N. Morris, 1898
MUSIC: Leila N. Morris, 1898

Purer in Heart 405

WORDS: Fannie C. Davidson, 1877
MUSIC: James H. Fillmore, 1877

406 Onward, Christian Soldiers

1. Onward, Christian soldiers, Marching as to war, With the cross of Jesus Going on before; Christ, the royal Master, Leads against the foe; Forward into battle, See His banners go!

2. At the name of Jesus, Satan's host doth flee; On, then, Christian soldiers, On to victory; Hell's foundations quiver At the shout of praise: Brother, lift your voices, Loud your anthems raise!

3. Crowns and thrones may perish, Kingdoms rise and wane, But the Church of Jesus Constant will remain; Gates of hell can never 'Gainst that church prevail; We have Christ's own promise, And that cannot fail.

4. Like a mighty army Moves the church of God; Brothers, we are treading Where the saints have trod. We are not divided, All one body we, One in hope and doctrine, One in charity.

5. Onward, then, ye people, Join our happy throng; Blend with ours your voices In the triumph song: "Glory, laud, and honor Unto Christ the King," This through countless ages Men and angels sing.

Onward, Christian soldiers! Marching as to war,

WORDS: Sabine Baring-Gould, 1864
MUSIC: Arthur Sullivan, 1871

Immortal, Invisible, God Only Wise 407

1. Im - mor - tal, in - vis - i - ble, God on - ly wise, In light in - ac - ces - si - ble hid from our eyes, Most bless - ed, most glo - rious, the An - cient of Days, Al - might - y, vic - to - rious, Thy great name we praise.
2. Un - rest - ing, un - hast - ing, and si - lent as light, Nor want - ing, nor wast - ing, Thou rul - est in might; Thy jus - tice like moun - tains high - soar - ing a - bove Thy clouds which are foun - tains of good - ness and love.
3. To all, life Thou giv - est, to both great and small; In all life Thou liv - est, the true life of all; Thy wis - dom so bound - less, Thy mer - cy so free, E - ter - nal Thy good - ness, for naught chang - eth Thee.
4. Great Fa - ther of Glo - ry, pure Fa - ther of Light, Thine an - gels a - dore Thee, all veil - ing their sight. All laud we would ren - der. O help us to see 'Tis on - ly the splen - dor of light hid - eth Thee.

WORDS: Walter Chalmers Smith, 1867
MUSIC: Traditional Welsh tune, 1839 (St. Denio)

410 When the Morning Comes

1. Tri - als dark on ev - 'ry hand, and we can - not un - der - stand All the ways that God will lead us to that bless - ed prom - ised land; But He'll guide us with His eye, and we'll fol - low till we die, We will un - der - stand it bet - ter by and by.
2. We are oft - en des - ti - tute of the things that life de - mands, Want of shel - ter and of food, thirst - y hills and bar - ren land; But we're trust - ing in the Lord, and ac - cord - ing to His word, We will un - der - stand it bet - ter by and by.
3. Temp - ta - tions, hid - den snares, oft - en take us un - a - wares, And our hearts are made to bleed for each thought - less word or deed; And we won - der why the test, when we try to do our best, But we'll un - der - stand it bet - ter by and by.

By and by, oh, when the morn - ing comes, All the saints of our

WORDS: Charles Tindley, 1905
MUSIC: Charles Tindley, 1905; arr. E. Sherwin Mackintosh, 1999

412 On Zion's Glorious Summit

1. On Zion's glorious summit stood a num'rous host redeemed by blood! They hymned their King in strains divine; I heard the song and strove to join, I heard the song and strove to join.
2. Here all who suffered sword or flame for truth, or Jesus' lovely name, shout vict'ry now and hail the Lamb, and bow before the great I AM, And bow before the great I AM.
3. While everlasting ages roll, eternal love shall feast their soul, and scenes of bliss, forever new, rise in succession to their view, Rise in succession to their view.

CODA
Holy, holy, holy Lord,

WORDS: John Kent, 1803
MUSIC: Robert Skene, 1869

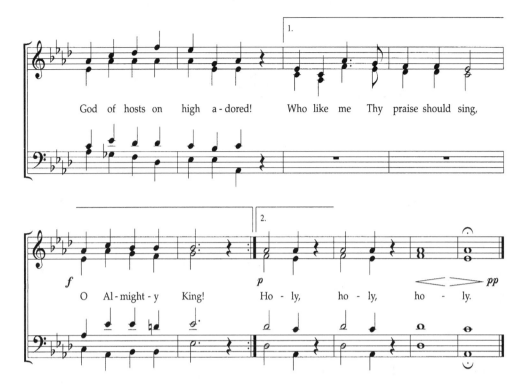

O Master, Let Me Walk with Thee 413

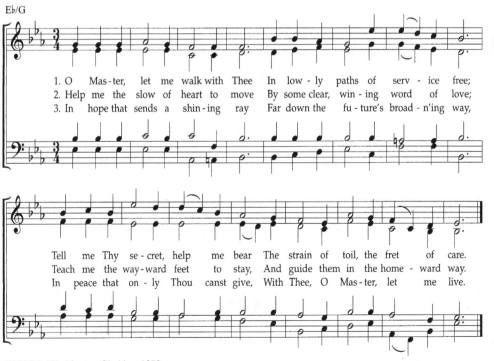

1. O Master, let me walk with Thee In lowly paths of service free; Tell me Thy secret, help me bear The strain of toil, the fret of care.
2. Help me the slow of heart to move By some clear, winning word of love; Teach me the wayward feet to stay, And guide them in the homeward way.
3. In hope that sends a shining ray Far down the future's broad'ning way, In peace that only Thou canst give, With Thee, O Master, let me live.

WORDS: Washington Gladden, 1879
MUSIC: Henry P. Smith, 1874

414 Love Lifted Me

WORDS: James Rowe, 1912
MUSIC: Howard E. Smith, 1912

Lord, We Come Before Thee Now 415

WORDS: William Hammond, 1749
MUSIC: Henri A. C. Malan, 1823; arr. Lowell Mason, 1841

416 Lo! What a Glorious Sight

WORDS: Isaac Watts, 1745
MUSIC: Jeremiah Ingalls, 1805

Jesus, Keep Me near the Cross 419

WORDS: Fanny J. Crosby, 1869
MUSIC: William H. Doane, 1869

420 I'll Be a Friend to Jesus

F/F

1. They tried my Lord and Master, With no one to defend; Within the halls of Pilate He stood without a friend.
2. The world may turn against Him, I'll love Him to the end, And while on earth I'm living, My Lord shall have a friend.
3. I'll do what He may bid me; I'll go where He may send; I'll try each flying moment To prove that I'm His friend.
4. To all who need a Savior, My Friend I recommend, Because He brought salvation, Is why I am His friend;

I'll be a friend to Jesus, My life for Him I'll spend; I'll be a friend to Jesus, Until my years shall end.

WORDS: Johnson Oatman, Jr., 1922
MUSIC: J. W. Dennis, 1922

Lead Me to Some Soul Today   421

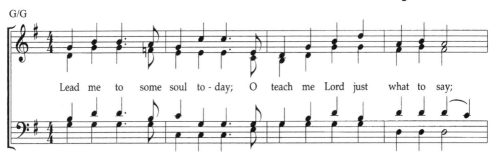

WORDS: Will Houghton, 1936
MUSIC: Wendell Loveless, 1936
© 1936. Renewed 1964 by Hope Publishing Co., Carol Stream, IL 60188. All rights reserved. Used by permission.

Jesus Is Lord

423

1. Jesus is Lord, my Redeemer; How He loves me, how I love Him; He is risen, He is risen, He is coming; Lord come quickly, Hallelujah! Lord come quickly, Hallelujah!
2. What a friend we have in Jesus, All our sins and griefs to bear; What a privilege to carry, What a privilege to carry Ev'rything to God in prayer. Ev'rything to God in prayer.
3. Hallelujah, hallelujah, Hallelujah, hallelujah; Hallelujah, hallelujah, He was born to die on Calvary To redeem a lost humanity. Suff'ring shame He rose triumphantly; Now He lives for all eternity. Lord come quickly Hallelujah! Lord come quickly Hallelujah!

WORDS: Traditional (verse 2: Joseph M. Scriven, 1855)
MUSIC: Traditional; arr. E. Sherwin Mackintosh

424 Jesus Loves Me!

1. Jesus loves me! This I know, For the Bible tells me so; Little ones to Him belong; They are weak but He is strong.
2. Jesus loves me! He who died, Heaven's gate to open wide; He will wash away my sin, Let His little child come in.
3. Jesus loves me! Love me still, Though I'm very weak and ill; From His shining throne on high, Comes to watch me where I lie.
4. Jesus loves the children dear, Children far away or near; They are safe when in His care, Ev'ry day and ev'rywhere.
5. Jesus, take this heart of mine, Make it pure and wholly Thine; Thou hast bled and died for me; I will henceforth live for Thee.
6. Jesus loves me! He will stay Close beside me all the way. He's prepared a house for me And someday His face I'll see.

Refrain: Yes, Jesus loves me; Yes, Jesus loves me; Yes, Jesus loves me; The Bible tells me so.

WORDS: Anna B. Warner, 1860
MUSIC: William B. Bradbury, 1862

I Know Whom I Have Believed 425

1. I know not why God's wondrous grace To me He hath made known,
2. I know not how the Spirit moves, Convincing men of sin,
3. I know not what of good or ill May be reserved for me,
4. I know not when my Lord may come, At night or noonday fair,

Nor why, unworthy, Christ in love, Redeemed me for His own.
Revealing Jesus through the word, Creating faith in Him.
Of weary ways or golden days, Before His face I see.
Nor if I'll walk the vale with Him, Or meet Him in the air.

But I know whom I have believed, And am persuaded that He is able To keep that which I've committed Unto Him against that day.

WORDS: Daniel W. Whittle, 1883 (based on 2 Timothy 1:12)
MUSIC: James McGranahan, 1883

427 Trust and Obey

1. When we walk with the Lord in the light of His Word, What a glory He sheds on our way! While we do His good will, He abides with us still, And with all who will trust and obey.
2. Not a burden we bear, not a sorrow we share, But our toil He doth richly repay; Not a grief nor a loss, not a frown nor a cross, But is blest if we trust and obey.
3. But we never can prove the delights of His love, Until all on the altar we lay; For the favor He shows, and the joy He bestows, Are for those who will trust and obey.
4. Then in fellowship sweet we will sit at His feet, Or we'll walk by His side in the way; What He says we will do, where He sends we will go, Never fear, only trust and obey.

Trust and obey, for there's no other way to be

WORDS: John H. Sammis, 1877
MUSIC: Daniel B. Towner, 1877

429 Lead Me to Calvary

Eb/G

1. King of my life, I crown Thee now, Thine shall the glory be;
2. Show me the tomb where Thou wast laid, Tenderly mourned and wept;
3. Let me like Mary, through the gloom, Come with a gift to Thee;
4. May I be willing, Lord, to bear Daily my cross for Thee;

Lest I forget Thy thorn-crowned brow, Lead me to Calvary.
Angels in robes of light arrayed Guarded Thee whilst Thou slept.
Show to me now the empty tomb, Lead me to Calvary.
Even Thy cup of grief to share, Thou hast borne all for me.

Lest I forget Gethsemane; Lest I forget Thine agony;

Lest I forget Thy love for me, lead me to Calvary.

WORDS: Jennie Evelyn Hussey, 1921
MUSIC: William J. Kirkpatrick, 1921

431 Alas! And Did My Savior Bleed?

1. Alas! And did my Savior bleed? And did my Sov'reign die? Would He devote that sacred head For such a one as I?
2. Was it for crimes that I have done, He groaned upon the tree? Amazing pity! Grace unknown! And love beyond degree!
3. Well might the sun in darkness hide, And shut his glories in, When Christ, the mighty Maker, died For man, the creature's sin.
4. But drops of grief can ne'er repay The debt of love I owe; Here, Lord, I give myself away, 'Tis all that I can do!

Chorus: At the cross, at the cross, where I first saw the light, And the burden of my heart rolled away, It was there by faith I received my sight, And now I am happy all the day!

WORDS: Isaac Watts, 1707 (verses); Ralph E. Hudson, 1885 (chorus)
MUSIC: Ralph E. Hudson, 1885

Have Thine Own Way 432

WORDS: Adelaide Pollard, 1902
MUSIC: George C. Stebbins, 1907

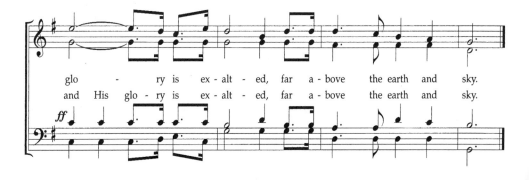

There's Not a Friend 435

WORDS: Johnson Oatman, Jr., 1895
MUSIC: George C. Hugg, 1895

437 Crown Him with Many Crowns

1. Crown Him with many crowns, The Lamb upon His throne; Hark, how the heav'nly anthem drowns All music but its own! Awake, my soul, and sing Of Him who died for thee, And hail Him as thy matchless King Through all eternity.

2. Crown Him the Lord of life, Who triumphed o'er the grave, Who rose victorious in the strife For those He came to save! His glories now we sing, Who died and rose on high, Who died eternal life to bring, And lives that death may die.

3. Crown Him the Lord of peace, Whose pow'r a scepter sways From pole to pole, that wars may cease, Absorbed in prayer and praise: His reign shall know no end, And round His pierced feet The fruits of Paradise extend, Their fragrance ever sweet.

4. Crown Him the Lord of heav'n, One with the Father known, And the blest Spirit, through Him giv'n From yonder glorious throne! All hail, Redeemer, hail! For Thou hast died for me; Thy praise and glory shall not fail Throughout eternity.

WORDS: Matthew Bridges, 1851 (verse 2: Godfrey Irving, 1874)
MUSIC: George J. Elvey, 1868

O Worship the King 438

1. O worship the King, all glorious above,
And gratefully sing His wonderful love;
Our Shield and Defender, the Ancient of Days,
Pavilioned in splendor and *girded with praise.

2. Thy bountiful care, what tongue can recite?
It breathes in the air, it shines in the light;
It streams from the hills, it descends to the plain,
And sweetly distills in the dew and the rain.

3. Frail children of dust, and feeble as frail,
In Thee do we trust, nor find Thee to fail;
Thy mercies, how tender! How firm to the end!
Our Maker, Defender, Redeemer, and Friend!

WORDS: Robert Grant, 1833
MUSIC: attr. J. Michael Haydn, 1815

("Girded" means surrounded or attached.)

439 Follow Me

WORDS: Ira F. Stanphill, 1953
MUSIC: Ira F. Stanphill, 1953

© 1953 Singspiration Music (ASCAP) (admin. by Brentwood-Benson Music Publishing, Inc., 365 Great Circle Rd., Nashville, TN 37228). All rights reserved. Used by permission.

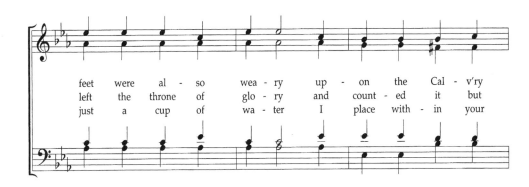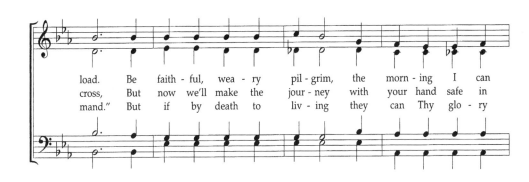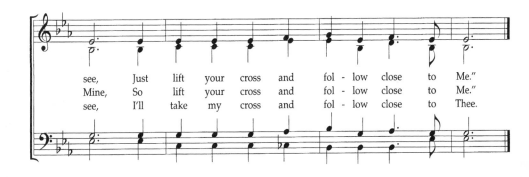

440 Sanctuary

WORDS: John Thompson and Randy Scruggs, 1982
MUSIC: John Thompson and Randy Scruggs, 1982 (descant: traditional)

Sing Hallelujah to the Lord 441

WORDS: Linda Stassen, 1974
MUSIC: Linda Stassen, 1974

442 Holy, Holy, Holy

Eb/Eb

1. Ho-ly, ho-ly, ho-ly! Lord God Al-might-y! Ear-ly in the morn-ing our song shall rise to Thee; Ho-ly, ho-ly, ho-ly! Mer-ci-ful and might-y! God o-ver all, and blest e-ter-nal-ly.
2. Ho-ly, ho-ly, ho-ly! All the saints a-dore Thee, cast-ing down their gold-en crowns a-round the crys-tal sea; Cher-u-bim and Ser-a-phim fall-ing down be-fore Thee, Who wast, and art, and ev-er-more shalt be.
3. Ho-ly, ho-ly, ho-ly! Though the dark-ness hide Thee, Though the eye of sin-ful man Thy glo-ry may not see; On-ly Thou art ho-ly! There is none be-side Thee, per-fect in pow'r, in love, and pur-i-ty.
4. Ho-ly, ho-ly, ho-ly! Lord God Al-might-y! All Thy works shall praise Thy name, in earth, and sky, and sea; Ho-ly, ho-ly, ho-ly! Mer-ci-ful and might-y! God o-ver all, and blest e-ter-nal-ly.

WORDS: Reginald Heber, 1826
MUSIC: John B. Dykes, 1861

444 Soldiers of Christ, Arise!

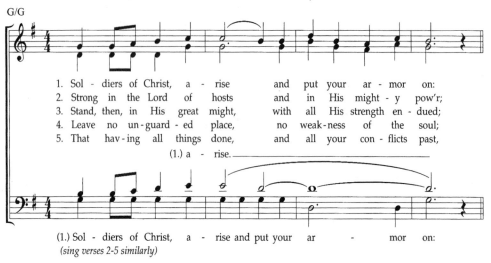

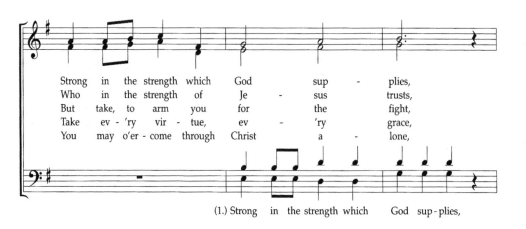

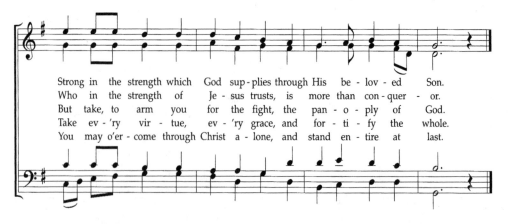

WORDS: Charles Wesley, 1749
MUSIC: William B. Bradbury, 1858

("Panoply" means full range.)

448 Just a Little Talk with Jesus

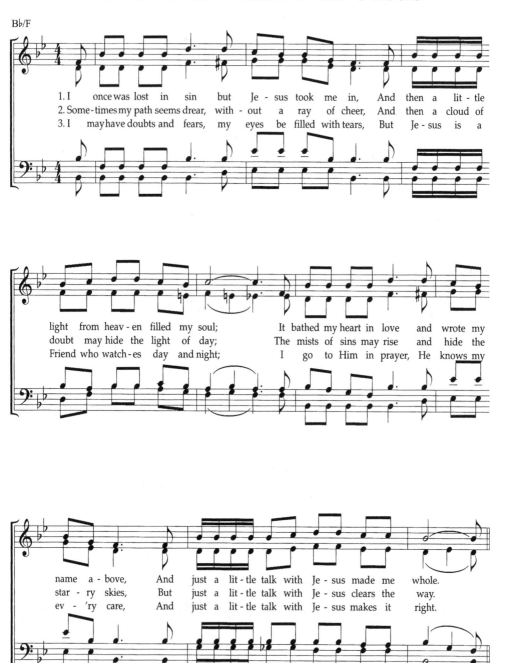

1. I once was lost in sin but Jesus took me in, And then a little light from heaven filled my soul; It bathed my heart in love and wrote my name above, And just a little talk with Jesus made me whole.

2. Sometimes my path seems drear, without a ray of cheer, And then a cloud of doubt may hide the light of day; The mists of sins may rise and hide the starry skies, But just a little talk with Jesus clears the way.

3. I may have doubts and fears, my eyes be filled with tears, But Jesus is a Friend who watches day and night; I go to Him in prayer, He knows my ev'ry care, And just a little talk with Jesus makes it right.

WORDS: Cleavant Derricks, 1937
MUSIC: Cleavant Derricks, 1937

449 I Will Sing the Wondrous Story

Eb/G

1. I will sing the wondrous story Of the Christ who died for me,
How He left His home in glory For the cross of Calvary.
2. I was lost, but Jesus found me, Found the sheep that went astray,
Threw His loving arms around me, Drew me back into His way.
3. I was bruised, but Jesus healed me; Faint was I from many' a fall;
Sight was gone, and fears possessed me, But He freed me from them all.
4. Days of darkness still come o'er me, Sorrow's paths I often tread,
But the Savior still is with me; By His hand I'm safely led.
5. He will keep me till the river Rolls its waters at my feet;
Then He'll bear me safely over, Where the loved ones I shall meet.

Refrain:
Yes, I'll sing the wondrous story Of the Christ who died for me,
Sing it with the saints in glory, Gathered by the crystal sea.

WORDS: Frances H. Rowley, 1886
MUSIC: Peter P. Bilhorn, 1886

Hallelujah! What a Savior! 450

1. "Man of Sorrows!" What a name for the Son of God who came
2. Bearing shame and scoffing rude, in my place condemned He stood
3. Guilty, vile and helpless we, spotless Lamb of God was He;
4. Lifted up was He to die, "It is finished!" was His cry;
5. When He comes, our glorious King, all His ransomed home to bring,

Ruined sinners to reclaim! Hallelujah! What a Savior!
Sealed my pardon with His blood: Hallelujah! What a Savior!
Full atonement! Can it be? Hallelujah! What a Savior!
Now in heav'n exalted high: Hallelujah! What a Savior!
Then anew this song we'll sing: Hallelujah! What a Savior!

WORDS: Philip P. Bliss, 1875
MUSIC: Philip P. Bliss, 1875

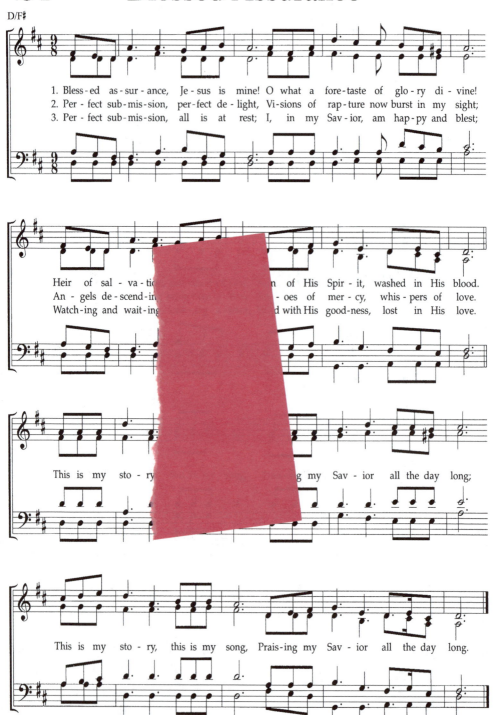

451 Blessed Assurance

1. Bless-ed as-sur-ance, Je-sus is mine! O what a fore-taste of glo-ry di-vine!
2. Per-fect sub-mis-sion, per-fect de-light, Vi-sions of rap-ture now burst in my sight;
3. Per-fect sub-mis-sion, all is at rest; I, in my Sav-ior, am hap-py and blest;

Heir of sal-va-tion, ... of His Spir-it, washed in His blood.
An-gels de-scend-ing ... -oes of mer-cy, whis-pers of love.
Watch-ing and wait-ing ... d with His good-ness, lost in His love.

This is my sto-ry, ... g my Sav-ior all the day long;
This is my sto-ry, this is my song, Prais-ing my Sav-ior all the day long.

WORDS: Fanny J. Crosby, 1873
MUSIC: Mrs. Joseph F. Knapp, 1873

Christ, the Lord, Is Risen Today 452

1. Christ, the Lord, is ris'n today, Hallelujah! Sons of men and angels say, Hallelujah! Raise your joys and triumphs high, Hallelujah! Sing, ye heav'ns; thou earth, reply, Hallelujah!
2. Love's redeeming work is done, Hallelujah! Fought the fight, the battle won, Hallelujah! Lo! Our sun's eclipse is o'er, Hallelujah! Lo! He sets in blood no more, Hallelujah!
3. Vain the stone, the watch, the seal, Hallelujah! Christ hath burst the gates of hell, Hallelujah! Death in vain forbids His rise, Hallelujah! Christ hath opened paradise, Hallelujah!
4. Lives again our glorious King, Hallelujah! Where, O death, is now thy sting? Hallelujah! Once He died our souls to save, Hallelujah! Where's thy vict'ry, boasting grave? Hallelujah!

WORDS: Charles Wesley, 1739
MUSIC: 14th century tune; revised in Walsh's "Lyra Davidica," 1708

453 Fairest Lord Jesus

Eb/Eb

1. Fair-est Lord Je-sus! Ru-ler of all na-ture!
O Thou of God and man the Son!
Thee will I cher-ish, Thee will I hon-or,
Thou, my soul's glo-ry, joy, and crown.

2. Fair are the mead-ows, fair-er still the wood-lands,
Robed in the bloom-ing garb of spring;
Je-sus is fair-er, Je-sus is pur-er,
Who makes the woe-ful heart to sing.

3. Fair is the sun-shine fair-er still the moon-light,
And all the twin-kling star-ry host:
Je-sus shines bright-er, Je-sus shines pur-er,
Than all the an-gels heav'n can boast.

4. Beau-ti-ful Sav-ior, Lord of all na-tions,
Son of God and Son of Man.
Glo-ry and hon-or, praise, ad-o-ra-tion
Now and for-ev-er-more be Thine.

WORDS: German hymn, 1677; trans. Richard S. Willis, 1850
MUSIC: Heinrich von Fallersleben; arr. Richard S. Willis, 1850

Beneath the Cross of Jesus 454

1. Beneath the cross of Jesus I fain would take my stand,
The shadow of a mighty rock within a weary land,
A home within the wilderness, a rest upon the way,
From the burning of the noontide heat, and the burden of the day.

2. O safe and happy shelter, O refuge tried and sweet,
O trysting place where heaven's love and heaven's justice meet!
As to the holy patriarch that wondrous dream was giv'n,
So seems my Savior's cross to me, a ladder up to heav'n.

3. Upon that cross of Jesus, mine eye at times can see
The very dying form of One who suffered there for me;
And from my smitten heart, with tears two wonders I confess:
The wonders of His glorious love, and my own worthlessness.

4. I take, O cross, thy shadow for my abiding place;
I ask no other sunshine than the sunshine of His face;
Content to let the world go by to know no gain nor loss,
My sinful self my only shame, my glory all the cross!

WORDS: Elizabeth C. Clephane, 1872 ("Fain" means gladly.)
MUSIC: Frederick C. Maker, 1881

455 Teach Me, Lord, to Wait

WORDS: Stuart Hamblen, 1953 (verse 3 based on Isaiah 40:31)
MUSIC: Stuart Hamblen, 1953; arr. E. Sherwin Mackintosh, 1999
© 1953. Renewed 1981. Hamblen Music Company. International copyright secured. All rights reserved.
Used by permission.

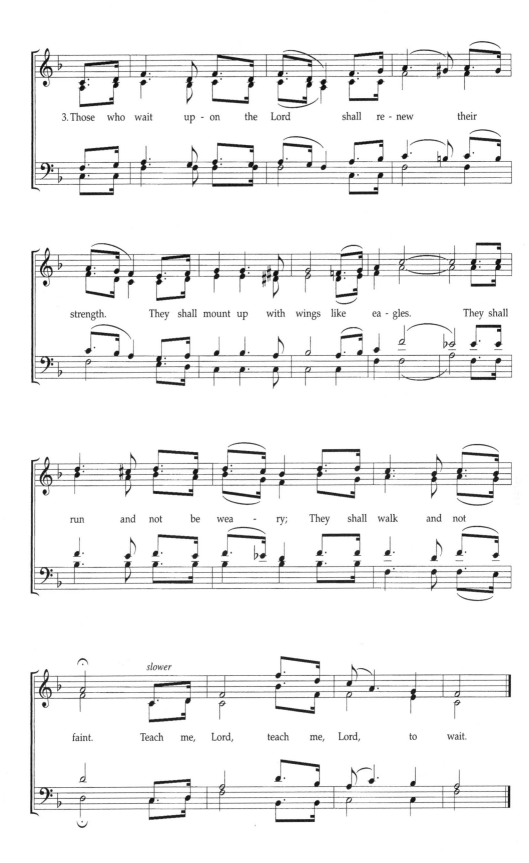

456 It Is Well with My Soul

1. When peace like a river attendeth my way, When sorrows like sea billows roll; Whatever my lot, Thou has taught me to say, "It is well, it is well with my soul."
2. My sin— O the bliss of this glorious thought— My sin, not in part, but the whole, Is nailed to the cross, and I bear it no more: Praise the Lord, praise the Lord, O my soul!
3. And, Lord, haste the day when the faith shall be sight, The clouds be rolled back as a scroll, The trump shall resound and the Lord shall descend, "Even so" it is well with my soul.

WORDS: Horatio G. Spafford, 1873 (verses 2, 4, 5 omitted)
MUSIC: Philip P. Bliss, 1876

When My Love to Christ Grows Weak 457

WORDS: John R. Wreford, 1837
MUSIC: Phoebe Palmer Knapp, 1908

458 Glory, Glory, Hallelujah!

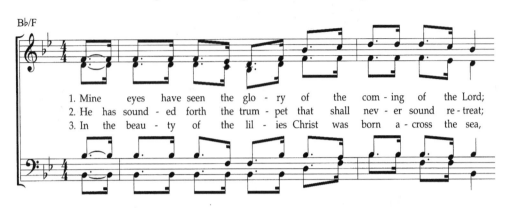

1. Mine eyes have seen the glory of the coming of the Lord;
2. He has sounded forth the trumpet that shall never sound retreat;
3. In the beauty of the lilies Christ was born across the sea,

He is trampling out the vintage where the grapes of wrath are stored;
He is sifting out the hearts of men before His judgment seat.
With a glory in His bosom that transfigures you and me;

He hath loosed the fateful lightning of His terrible swift sword;
O be swift, my soul, to answer Him, be jubilant, my feet!
As He died to make men holy, let us die to make men free;

WORDS: Julia Ward Howe, 1862
MUSIC: William Steffe, 1852; descant: traditional

459 We're Marching to Zion

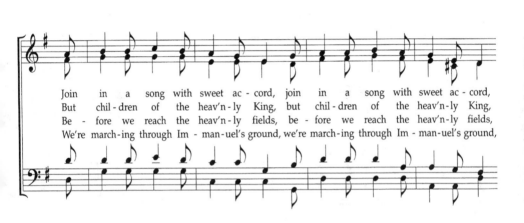
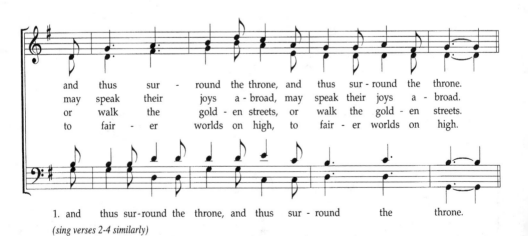

1. Come, we that love the Lord, and let our joys be known; join in a song with sweet accord, join in a song with sweet accord, and thus surround the throne, and thus surround the throne.
2. Let those refuse to sing who never knew our God; but children of the heav'nly King, but children of the heav'nly King, may speak their joys abroad, may speak their joys abroad.
3. The hill of Zion yields a thousand sacred sweets, before we reach the heav'nly fields, before we reach the heav'nly fields, or walk the golden streets, or walk the golden streets.
4. Then let our songs abound, and ev'ry tear be dry; we're marching through Immanuel's ground, we're marching through Immanuel's ground, to fairer worlds on high, to fairer worlds on high.

(sing verses 2-4 similarly)

WORDS: Isaac Watts, 1707
MUSIC: Robert Lowery, 1867

I'm Not Ashamed to Own My Lord   460

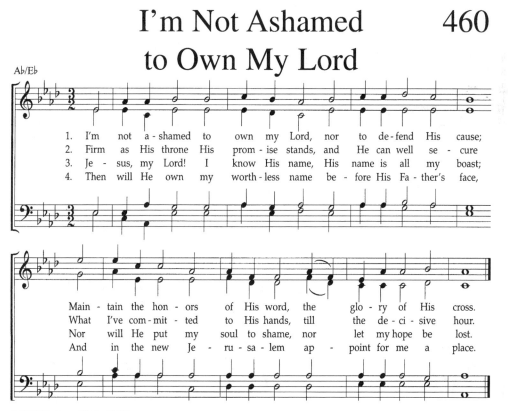

1. I'm not a-shamed to own my Lord, nor to de-fend His cause;
   Main-tain the hon-ors of His word, the glo-ry of His cross.
2. Firm as His throne His prom-ise stands, and He can well se-cure
   What I've com-mit-ted to His hands, till the de-ci-sive hour.
3. Je-sus, my Lord! I know His name, His name is all my boast;
   Nor will He put my soul to shame, nor let my hope be lost.
4. Then will He own my worth-less name be-fore His Fa-ther's face,
   And in the new Je-ru-sa-lem ap-point for me a place.

WORDS: Isaac Watts, 1707
MUSIC: Carl G. Glaser, 1839; arr. Lowell Mason, 1839

I Know That My Redeemer Lives 462

WORDS: Fred A. Fillmore, 1917 (based on Job 19:25)
MUSIC: Fred A. Fillmore, 1917

463 My Hope Is Built

1. My hope is built on nothing less Than Jesus' blood and righteousness; I dare not trust the sweetest frame, But wholly lean on Jesus' name.
2. When darkness veils His lovely face, I rest on His unchanging grace; In ev'ry high and stormy gale, My anchor holds within the veil.
3. His oath, His covenant, His blood, Support me in the whelming flood; When all around my soul gives way, He then is all my hope and stay.
4. When He shall come with trumpet sound, O may I then in Him be found, Dressed in His righteousness alone, Faultless to stand before the throne.

Refrain: On Christ, the Solid Rock, I stand, all other ground is sinking sand, all other ground is sinking sand.

WORDS: Edward Mote, 1834
MUSIC: William B. Bradbury, 1863

465 Be Still, My Soul

1. Be still, my soul, the Lord is on thy side; Bear patiently the cross of grief or pain. Leave to thy God to order and provide; In ev'ry change He faithful will remain. Be still, my soul, thy best, thy heav'nly Friend Through thorny ways leads to a joyful end.

2. Be still, my soul, thy God doth undertake To guide the future as He has the past. Thy hope, thy confidence let nothing shake; All now mysterious shall be bright at last. Be still, my soul, the waves and winds still know His voice who ruled them while He dwelt below.

3. Be still, my soul, the hour is hast'ning on When we shall be forever with the Lord. When disappointment, grief, and fear are gone; Sorrow forgot, love's purest joys restored. Be still, my soul, when change and tears are past, All safe and blessed we shall meet at last.

WORDS: Katharina von Schlege, 1752; trans. Jane Borthwick, 1855
MUSIC: Jean Sibelius, 1899

467 My God and I

First verse: Sopranos sing words, others "oo"
Second verse: Altos sing words, others "oo"
Third verse: Basses sing words, others "oo"
All voices sings words at "All"
WORDS: I. B. Sergai (Austris A. Wihtol), 1935
MUSIC: I. B. Sergai (Austris A. Wihtol); arr. E. Sherwin Mackintosh, 1992
© 1935 Singspiration Music (ASCAP) (admin. by Brentwood-Benson Music Publishing, Inc., 365 Great Circle Rd., Nashville, TN 37228). All rights reserved. Used by permission.

All: We clasp our hands, our voices ring with laughter,
All: When all was but a dream of dim conception,
All: This earth will pass, and with it common trifles,

My God and I walk through the meadow's hue.
To come to life, earth's verdant glory see.
But God and I will go unendingly.

Breathe on Me, Breath of God   468

1. Breathe on me, breath of God, Fill me with life anew,
2. Breathe on me, breath of God, Until my heart is pure,
3. Breathe on me, breath of God, Till I am wholly Thine,
4. Breathe on me, breath of God, So shall I never die,

That I may love what Thou dost love, And do what Thou wouldst do.
Until with Thee I will one will, To do and to endure.
Till all this earthly part of me Glows with Thy fire divine.
But live with Thee the perfect life Of Thine eternity.

WORDS: Edwin Hatch, 1878
MUSIC: Robert Jackson, 1874

469 Low in the Grave He Lay

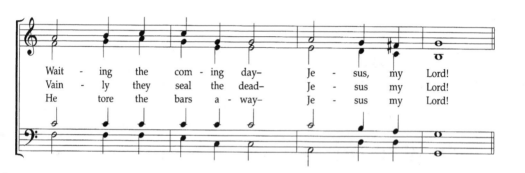

WORDS: Robert Lowry, 1874
MUSIC: Robert Lowry, 1874

For the Beauty of the Earth 470

WORDS: Folliot S. Pierpoint, 1864
MUSIC: Conrad Kocher, 1838; adpt. W. H. Monk, 1861

471. Just As I Am

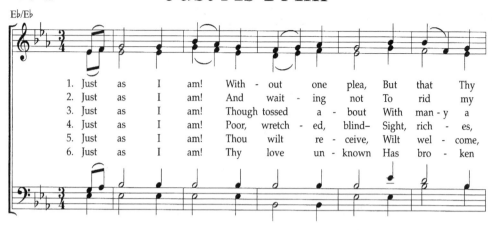

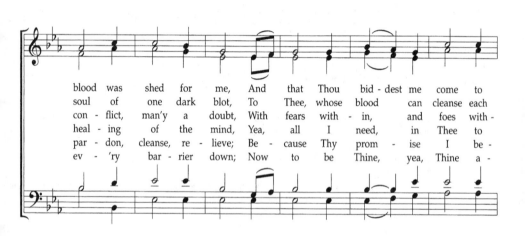

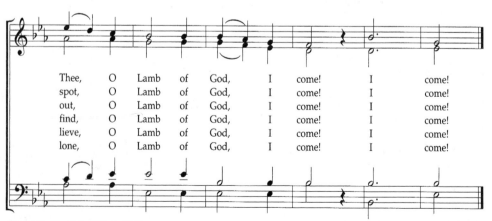

WORDS: Charlotte Elliott, 1834
MUSIC: William Bradbury, 1849

Just a Closer Walk with Thee 472

1. I am weak, but Thou art strong; Jesus, keep me from all wrong.
2. Through this world of toil and snares, If I falter, Lord, who cares?
3. When my feeble life is o'er, Time for me will be no more.

I'll be satisfied as long As I walk, dear Lord, close to Thee.
Who with me my burden shares? None but Thee, dear Lord, none but Thee.
Guide me gently, safely o'er To Thy kingdom shore, to Thy shore.

Just a closer walk with Thee, Grant it, Jesus, is my plea.

Daily walking close to Thee, Let it be, dear Lord, let it be.

WORDS: American folk song
MUSIC: American folk song; arr. Mosie Lister

All to Jesus I Surrender 474

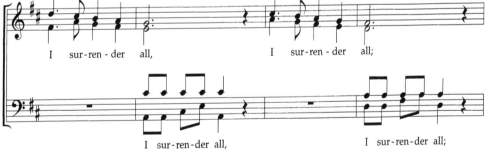

WORDS: Judson W. Van De Venter, 1896
MUSIC: Winfield S. Weeden, 1896

475 Christ, We Do All Adore Thee

WORDS: Theodore Baker, 1927
MUSIC: Theodore Dubois, 1866

All Hail the Power   476

1. All hail the pow'r of Jesus' name! Let angels prostrate fall!
Bring forth the royal diadem, and crown Him Lord of all;
Bring forth the royal diadem, and crown Him Lord of all.

2. Ye chosen seed of Israel's race, ye ransomed from the fall,
Hail Him who saves you by His grace, and crown Him Lord of all;
Hail Him who saves you by His grace, and crown Him Lord of all.

3. Let ev'ry kindred, ev'ry tribe, on this terrestrial ball,
To Him all majesty ascribe, and crown Him Lord of all;
To Him all majesty ascribe, and crown Him Lord of all.

4. O that with yonder sacred throng we at His feet may fall!
We'll join the everlasting song, and crown Him Lord of all;
We'll join the everlasting song, and crown Him Lord of all.

WORDS: Edward Perronet, 1780; adpt. John Rippen, 1787
MUSIC: Oliver Holden, 1793 ("Coronation")

477 Lord, Speak to Me

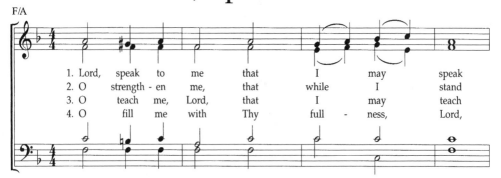

1. Lord, speak to me that I may speak
2. O strengthen me, that while I stand
3. O teach me, Lord, that I may teach
4. O fill me with Thy fullness, Lord,

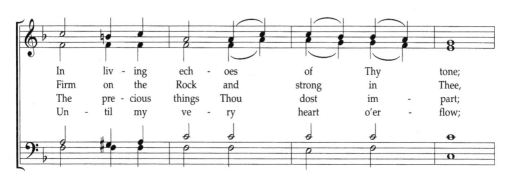

In living echoes of Thy tone;
Firm on the Rock and strong in Thee,
The precious things Thou dost impart;
Until my very heart o'erflow;

As Thou has sought, so let me seek
I may stretch out a loving hand
And wing my words that they may reach
In kindling thought and glowing word,

Thine erring children, lost and 'lone.
To wrestlers with the troubled sea.
The hidden depths of man'y a heart.
Thy love to tell, Thy praise to show.

WORDS: Frances R. Havergal, 1872
MUSIC: George Hews, 1835

550 O Come, All Ye Faithful

WORDS: Latin hymn; ascr. John Francis Wade, 1751; trans. Frederick Oakeley, 1841, W. T. Brook et. al.
MUSIC: John Francis Wade's *Cantus Diversi*, 1751

O Come, O Come, Emmanuel 551

1. O come, O come, Emmanuel And ransom captive Israel, That mourns in lonely exile here Until the Son of God appear.
2. O come, Thou Wisdom from on high And order all things far and nigh. To us the path of knowledge show; And cause us in Thy way to go.
3. O come, Desire of Nations, bind All peoples in one heart and mind, Bid envy, strife and quarrels cease; Fill the whole world with heaven's peace.

Rejoice! Rejoice! Emmanuel shall come to thee, O Israel!

WORDS: Traditional
MUSIC: Gregorian chant (15th century French Franciscan processional); arr. E. Sherwin Mackintosh, 1999
[Paris, Bib. Nat. Fonds Latin MS 10581]

It Came upon the Midnight Clear 553

1. It came upon the midnight clear, That glorious song of old, From angels bending near the earth To touch their harps of gold: "Peace on the earth, good-will to men, From heav'n's all-gracious King;" The world in solemn stillness lay To hear the angels sing.

2. Still through the cloven skies they come, With peaceful wings unfurled, And still their heav'nly music floats O'er all the weary world; Above its sad and lowly plains They bend on hov'ring wing, And ever, o'er its 'Babel sounds,' The blessed angels sing.

3. Yet with the woes of sin and strife The world has suffered long; Beneath the angel-strain have rolled Two thousand years of wrong; And men, at war with men, hear not The love-song which they bring: O hush the noise, ye men of strife, Which now the angels sing.

4. For lo! The days are hast'ning on, By prophets seen of old, When with the ever-circling years, Shall come the time foretold, When the whole heav'n and earth shall own The Prince of Peace their King, And the whole world send back the song Which now the angels sing.

WORDS: Edward H. Sears, 1849
MUSIC: Richard S. Willis, 1850

554 Angels We Have Heard on High

1. Angels we have heard on high, Sweetly singing o'er the plain (And) And the mountains in reply Echo back their joyous strain: Gloria in excelsis Deo, (Oh,) Gloria
2. Come to Bethlehem and see, Him whose birth the angels sing, (Come) Come adore on bended knee Christ the Lord, the new-born King.

WORDS: French carol
MUSIC: French carol; arr. E. Sherwin Mackintosh

("Gloria in excelsis Deo" means glory to God in the highest.)

Silent Night

556

1. Si - lent night, ho - ly night! All is calm, all is bright
2. Si - lent night, ho - ly night! Shep - herds quake at the sight;
3. Si - lent night, ho - ly night! Son of God, love's pure light;

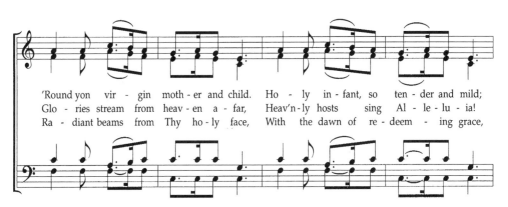

'Round yon vir - gin moth - er and child. Ho - ly in - fant, so ten - der and mild;
Glo - ries stream from heav - en a - far, Heav'n - ly hosts sing Al - le - lu - ia!
Ra - diant beams from Thy ho - ly face, With the dawn of re - deem - ing grace,

Sleep in heav - en - ly peace, Sleep in heav - en - ly peace!
Christ the Sav - ior is born, Christ the Sav - ior is born!
Je - sus, Lord at Thy birth, Je - sus, Lord at Thy birth!

WORDS: Joseph Mohr; trans. John F. Young
MUSIC: Franz Grüber

557 Hark! The Herald Angels Sing

1. Hark! The herald angels sing: "Glory to the newborn King!
Peace on earth and mercy mild, God and sinners reconciled!"
Joyful all ye nations rise, Join the triumph of the skies;
With th' angelic host proclaim: "Christ is born in Bethlehem!"

2. Christ, by highest heav'n adored; Christ, the everlasting Lord;
Late in time behold Him come, Offspring of the virgin's womb.
Veiled in flesh the Godhead see; Hail th' Incarnate Deity,
Pleased as Man with men to dwell; Jesus, our Emmanuel!

3. Hail the heav'n-born Prince of Peace, Hail the Sun of Righteousness!
Light and life to all He brings, Ris'n with healing in His wings.
Mild, He lays His glory by, Born that man no more may die,
Born to raise the sons of earth, Born to give them second birth.

WORDS: Charles Wesley, 1739
MUSIC: Felix Mendelssohn, 1840; arr. William H. Cunnings, 1856

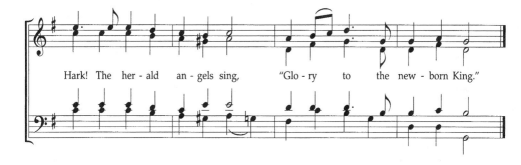

Isaiah 9:2, 6-7

The people walking in darkness
 have seen a great light;
on those living in the land of the
  shadow of death
 a light has dawned....
For to us a child is born,
 to us a son is given,
  and the government will be on his
   shoulders.
And he will be called
 Wonderful Counselor, Mighty God,
 Everlasting Father, Prince of Peace.
Of the increase of his government
  and peace
 there will be no end.
He will reign on David's throne
 and over his kingdom,
establishing and upholding it
 with justice and righteousness
 from that time on and forever.
The zeal of the Lord Almighty
 will accomplish this.

Spiritual Songs

Lord, I Thank You 600

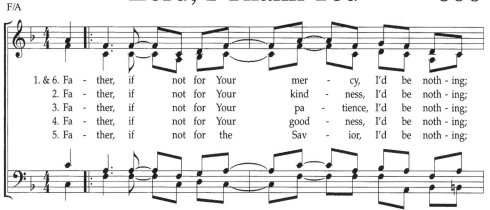

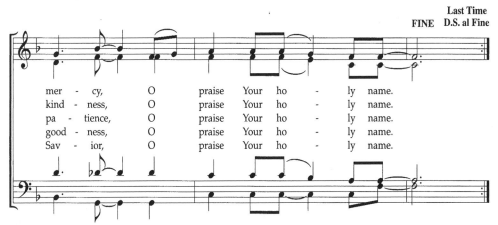

WORDS: David E. Finnell, 1988
MUSIC: David E. Finnell, 1988
© 1988 Discipleship Publications International. All rights reserved.

601 Lord God Almighty

*Other verses: love, serve, give, preach, etc.
WORDS: Daniel Macaluso, 1989
MUSIC: Daniel Macaluso, 1989; arr. E. Sherwin Mackintosh, 1999
© 1989 Discipleship Publications International. All rights reserved. Used by permission.

Translation:
One of these days the Lord Jesus will come back.
We will clap (poketela) our hands with Him.
We will walk (fama fama) with Him.
We will dance (cheena cheena) with Him.
We will sing "Hosanna" (yimbelela "Hosana").
WORDS: Traditional Shongan hymn
MUSIC: Traditional Shongan hymn; arr. by E. Sherwin Mackintosh
© 1995 New York City Church of Christ. All rights reserved. Used by permission.

604 The Glory Song

WORDS: Luis J. Martinez, 1995
MUSIC: Traditional; arr. Luis J. Martinez, 1995
© 1995 Los Angeles International Church of Christ. All rights reserved. Used by permission.

2. From thirty came three hundred then three thousand; Chicago, New York, Paris, London; Mexico, Tokyo, Johannesburg; Bombay and Hong Kong and Cairo—the world! By making disciples in the name of the Son, Restoration led to Revolution!

3. They called the Remnant to reconstruction—the Kingdom brotherhood had begun. "Church" became "family" and opened the door, and HOPE worldwide would remember the poor. The winds o' change were blowin' that "Salvation is now!" In 1991 we planted Moscow.

4. A world divided by race and hate—millions continue right through hell's gate. Riots and death had come to L.A., but the Lord our God would have the last say. Now down in South Central, kinda like a grenade, they call it the Cross and the Switchblade!

5. From the days of the Baptist, the prophet John, the kingdom of Heaven keeps pushin' on. Through forceful men and women who dream, whether single or married, college or teen! Fillin' the world's great auditoriums, the dream of the Super Church has come!

6. The Word of our God cuts like a knife—it's the power of the Lord to change your life. We fellowship, break bread and help those astray, and He adds to our numbers every day! In Jakarta, Manila, Milan and B.A., families are reconciled because we pray!

7. Someday, in heaven, we'll gather around the throne of our God, and we'll all bow down. Though brothers and sisters had died for Christ, we all knew it was worth the sacrifice. And around the throne we're gonna sing and say, "The world was evangelized in our day!"

605 In the Kingdom

Am/A

1. Are you stand-ing in the place that will stand for-ev-er? Stand-ing,
2. Are you walk-ing on the road that will lead to heav-en? Walk-ing,
3. Are you look-ing at the light that will shine for-ev-er? Look-ing,
4. Are you shar-ing the word that you can share for-ev-er? Shar-ing,

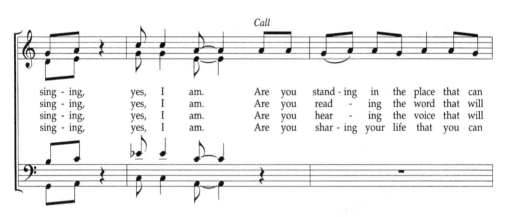

sing-ing, yes, I am. Are you stand-ing in the place that can
sing-ing, yes, I am. Are you read-ing the word that will
sing-ing, yes, I am. Are you hear-ing the voice that will
sing-ing, yes, I am. Are you shar-ing your life that you can

stand the weath-er? Stand-ing, sing-ing, yes, I am.
read for-ev-er? Read-ing, sing-ing, yes, I am.
ring for-ev-er? Hear-ing, sing-ing, yes, I am.
share for-ev-er? Shar-ing, sing-ing, yes, I am.

WORDS: Larry Jackson, 1989
MUSIC: Larry Jackson, 1989
© 1989 Discipleship Publications International. All rights reserved.

606   He's On Time

WORDS: Rob Milner
MUSIC: Rob Milner
Copyright © 2006 by Rob Milner. Licensed from River City Music, LLC.

607 Home in Heaven

WORDS: J. Brian Craig
MUSIC: J. Brian Craig
Copyright © 1998 by J. Brian Craig. Licensed from River City Music, LLC.

608 I'm Building Me A Home

WORDS: Traditional
MUSIC: Traditional. Arr. by S. Chase Mackintosh and E. Sherwin Mackintosh
Copyright © 2010 by E. Sherwin Mackintosh. Licensed from River City Music, LLC.

609 I'm Going to Praise You

1. I'm gon-na praise You with my song, gon-na praise You with my spir-it.
2. I'm gon-na praise You with my heart, gon-na praise You with my spir-it.
3. I'm gon-na praise You with my soul, gon-na praise You with my spir-it.
4. I'm gon-na praise You with my mind, gon-na praise You with my spir-it.
5. I'm gon-na praise You with my strength, gon-na praise You with my spir-it.

Gon-na praise You with my song, gon-na praise You all day long.
Gon-na praise You with my heart, You've been with me from the start.
Gon-na praise You with my soul, on-ly You can make me whole.
Gon-na praise You with my mind, gon-na praise You all the time.
Gon-na praise You with my strength, gon-na with ev-'ry-thing.

O God, hear my call. O God, lift me high-er.

O God, hear my call. Lift me up so I can sing Your praise.

WORDS: J. Brian Craig
MUSIC: J. Brian Craig
Copyright © 2005 by J. Brian Craig. Licensed from River City Music, LLC.

If You Want to Love Him   610

WORDS: Brad Klump
MUSIC: Brad Klump
Copyright © 2000 by Brad Klump. Licensed from River City Music, LLC.

700 Thank You, Lord

1. Thank You, Lord, for lov-ing me; and thank You, Lord, for bless-ing me.
2. Let us all with one ac-cord sing prais - es to Christ the Lord.
3. Please re - veal Your will for me so I can serve You for e - ter - ni - ty.

Thank You, Lord, for mak-ing me whole and sav - ing my soul.
Let us all u - nite in song and praise Him all day long.
Use my life in ev - 'ry way, take hold of it to - day.

Thank You, Lord, for lov-ing me. Thank You, Lord, for sav - ing my soul.

WORDS: Gary L. Mabry, 1972
MUSIC: Gary L. Mabry, 1972; arr. E. Sherwin Mackintosh, 1999
© 1972 Gary L. Mabry / 1974 Sweet Publishing Company in REJOICE! and SING TO THE LORD.
All rights reserved. Used by permission.

Psalm 118:21-24

I will give you thanks, for you answered me;
    you have become my salvation.
The stone the builders rejected
    has become the capstone;
the Lord has done this,
    and it is marvelous in our eyes.
This is the day the Lord has made;
    let us rejoice and be glad in it.

Amen 701

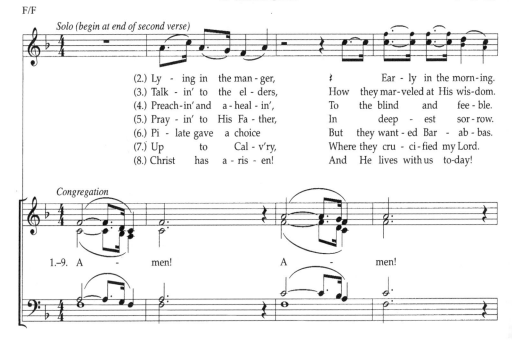

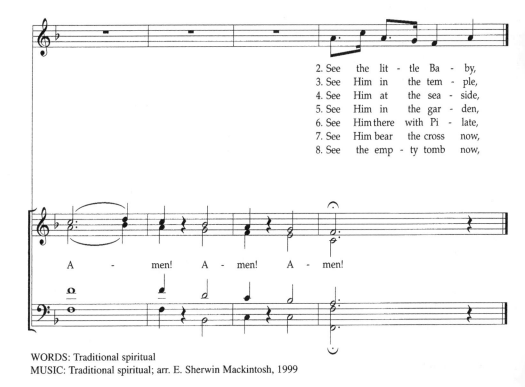

WORDS: Traditional spiritual
MUSIC: Traditional spiritual; arr. E. Sherwin Mackintosh, 1999

E-Khaya
(Hallelujah!)

703

F/C

Translation (Zulu): "Hallelujah! Jesus is coming soon!"
WORDS: Traditional
MUSIC: Traditional; arr. E. Sherwin Mackintosh, 1999

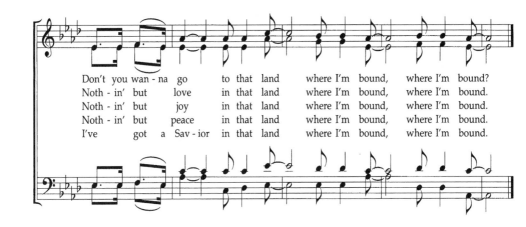

God Is So Good 706

WORDS: Traditional
MUSIC: Traditional; arr. E. Sherwin Mackintosh, 1999

708 Hard Fighting Soldier

Ab/Eb

Chorus: Lord, I'm a hard fighting soldier on the battlefield. Lord, I'm a hard fighting soldier on the battlefield. Lord, I'm a hard fighting soldier on the battlefield.

1. I've got a helmet on my head and in my hand a sword and shield. I've got a helmet on my head and in my hand a sword and shield. I've got a helmet on my head and in my hand a sword and shield. I got the word for my sword and I got

2. You've gotta walk right and talk right and sing right and pray right on the battlefield. You've gotta walk right and talk right and sing right and pray right on the battlefield. You've gotta walk right and talk right and sing right and pray right

3. You know that Jesus is my Captain and He fights my battles still; He has never lost a battle and I know He never will. I

4. And when I die, let me die in the service of my Lord. And when I die, let me die in the service of my Lord. And when I die, let me die in the

WORDS: Traditional
MUSIC: Traditional; arr. E. Sherwin Mackintosh, 1999

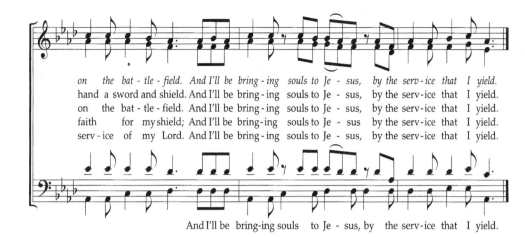

He Is Lord! 709

WORDS: Traditional (verse 2 by Alton Howard, 1992)
MUSIC: Traditional

710 I Am a Poor Wayfaring Stranger

WORDS: American folk song (Bever's Christian Songster, 1858)
MUSIC: American folk song (Tillman's Revival, 1891); arr. E. Sherwin Mackintosh, 1999

Glory, Glory

(Laid My Burdens Down)

711

WORDS: Traditional
MUSIC: Traditional; arr. E. Sherwin Mackintosh, 1999

712 I Can't Keep It to Myself

*For additional verses use "sing," "preach," "shout," etc.
WORDS: Traditional
MUSIC: Traditional; arr. E. Sherwin Mackintosh, 1999

I Feel Good 714

*For additional verses use "love," "joy," "peace," etc.
WORDS: Lanny Wolfe, 1977
MUSIC: Lanny Wolfe, 1977
© 1977 Lanny Wolfe Music / ASCAP (admin. by ICG, Inc. P. O. Box 24149, Nashville, TN 37202.) All rights reserved. Used by permission.

715 I Want Jesus to Walk with Me

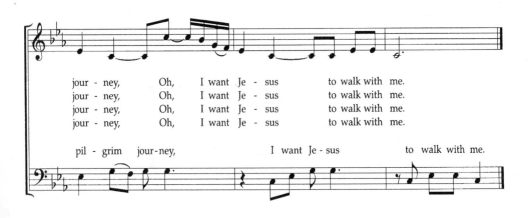

1. I want Jesus to walk with me, I want Jesus to walk with me; All along life's pilgrim journey, Oh, I want Jesus to walk with me.
2. In my trials, He'll walk with me, In my trials, He'll walk with me; All along life's pilgrim journey, Oh, I want Jesus to walk with me.
3. In my sorrows, He'll walk with me, In my sorrows, He'll walk with me; All along life's pilgrim journey, Oh, I want Jesus to walk with me.
4. I love Jesus and He loves me, I love Jesus and He loves me; All along life's pilgrim journey, Oh, I want Jesus to walk with me.

WORDS: Traditional
MUSIC: Traditional

719 Jesus Will Fix It

*For additional verses use "fight," "cry," "sing," etc.
WORDS: Traditional
MUSIC: Traditional; arr. E. Sherwin Mackintosh, 1999

720 Let Your Living Water Flow

1.,3. Let Your living water flow over my soul. Let Your Holy Spirit come and take control Of ev-'ry situation that troubles my mind. All my cares and burdens onto You I roll.

2. Give Your life to Jesus, let Him fill your soul. Let Him take you in His arms and make you whole. As you give your life to Him, He'll set you free: You will live and reign with Him eternally.

Jesus, Jesus; Je-
Father, Father; Fa-
Spirit, Spirit; Spir-

WORDS: John Watson, 1982
MUSIC: John Watson, 1982; arr. E. Sherwin Mackintosh, 1999
© 1982 Ampelos Music (admin. by The Copyright Company, 40 Music Sq. E, Nashville, TN 37203).
International copyright secured. All rights reserved. Used by permission.

Let Us Break Bread Together 721

WORDS: Traditional
MUSIC: Traditional; arr. E. Sherwin Mackintosh, 1999

722 I Love to Praise His Holy Name

WORDS: Traditional
MUSIC: Traditional; arr. E. Sherwin Mackintosh, 1999

*Or: 'Jewel'

723 Love, Love, Love

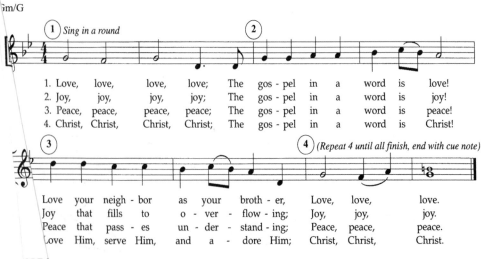

1. Love, love, love, love; The gospel in a word is love!
2. Joy, joy, joy, joy; The gospel in a word is joy!
3. Peace, peace, peace, peace; The gospel in a word is peace!
4. Christ, Christ, Christ, Christ; The gospel in a word is Christ!

(Repeat 4 until all finish, end with cue note)

Love your neighbor as your brother, Love, love, love.
Joy that fills to overflowing; Joy, joy, joy.
Peace that passes understanding; Peace, peace, peace.
Love Him, serve Him, and adore Him; Christ, Christ, Christ.

WORDS: Traditional
MUSIC: Traditional

There Is a Balm in Gilead 724

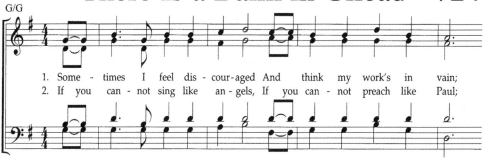
1. Some-times I feel dis-cour-aged And think my work's in vain;
2. If you can-not sing like an-gels, If you can-not preach like Paul;

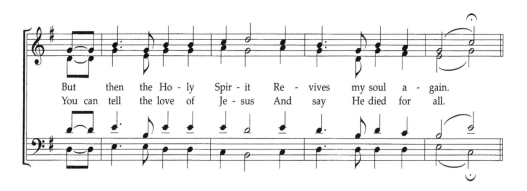
But then the Ho-ly Spir-it Re-vives my soul a-gain.
You can tell the love of Je-sus And say He died for all.

There is a balm in Gil-e-ad, To make the wound-ed whole.
(There is a balm)

There is a balm in Gil-e-ad, To heal the sin-sick soul.
(There is a balm)

WORDS: Traditional ("Gilead" is a region in Israel famous for medicine [balm].)
MUSIC: Traditional; arr. E. Sherwin Mackintosh, 1999

725 I've Been Redeemed

WORDS: Traditional
MUSIC: Traditional; arr. E. Sherwin Mackintosh, 1999

WORDS: Traditional
MUSIC: Traditional; arr. E. Sherwin Mackintosh, 1999

Sign Me Up 728

WORDS: Traditional
MUSIC: Traditional; arr. E. Sherwin Mackintosh, 1999

729 Jordan River

WORDS: Traditional
MUSIC: Traditional spiritual; arr. E. Sherwin Mackintosh, 1999

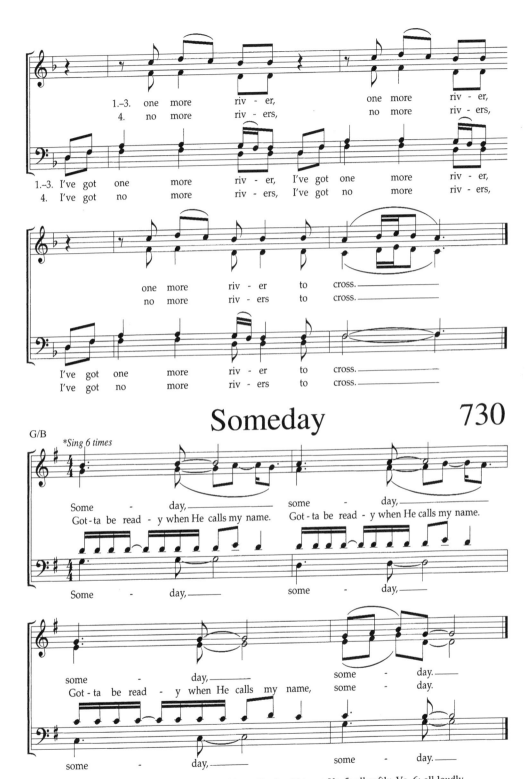

Someday 730

*Vs. 1: soprano only, Vs. 2: add alto, Vs. 3: add bass, Vs. 4: add tenor, Vs. 5: all softly, Vs. 6: all loudly
WORDS: Traditional
MUSIC: Traditional; arr. Jon Augustine, 1999

Swing Low, Sweet Chariot 732

WORDS: Traditional Spiritual
MUSIC: Traditional; arr. E. Sherwin Mackintosh, 1999

733 Take the Lord with You
Ab/C

1. You've got to take the Lord with you, chil-dren, ev-'ry-where you
2. You've got to make dis-ci-ples dai-ly, chil-dren, ev-'ry-where you
3. You've got to love your broth-ers dai-ly, chil-dren, ev-'ry-where you

go. You've got to take the Lord with you, chil-dren, ev-'ry-where you
go. You've got to make dis-ci-ples dai-ly, chil-dren, ev-'ry-where you
go. You've got to love your broth-ers dai-ly, chil-dren, ev-'ry-where you

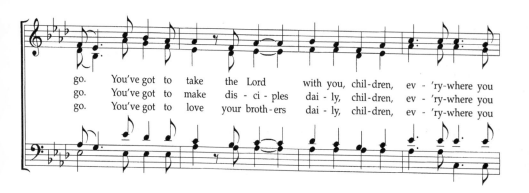

go. You've got to take the Lord with you, chil-dren, ev-'ry-where you
go. You've got to make dis-ci-ples dai-ly, chil-dren, ev-'ry-where you
go. You've got to love your broth-ers dai-ly, chil-dren, ev-'ry-where you

WORDS: Traditional
MUSIC: Traditional; arr. E. Sherwin Mackintosh

734 Wade in the Water

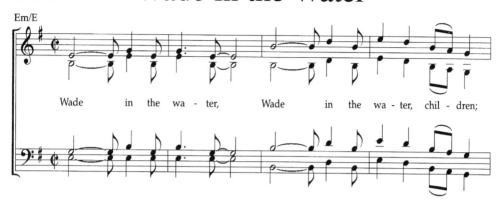

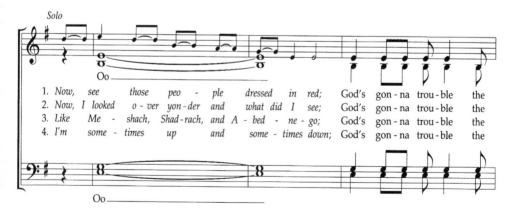

WORDS: Traditional (verses by Richard Washington)
MUSIC: Traditional; arr. by Richard Washington and E. Sherwin Mackintosh, 1999

735 Were You There?

1. Were you there when they cru-ci-fied my Lord?
2. Were you there when they nailed Him to the tree?
3. Were you there when they laid Him in the tomb? (Were you there?)
4. Were you there when He rose to live a-gain?

Were you there when they cru-ci-fied my Lord?
Were you there when they nailed Him to the tree?
Were you there when they laid Him in the tomb? (Were you there?)
Were you there when He rose to live a-gain?

Oh! Some-times it caus-es me to trem-ble, trem-ble, trem-ble. Were you

WORDS: Traditional
MUSIC: Traditional spiritual; adpt. John W. Work Jr./Frederick J. Work; arr. E. Sherwin Mackintosh, 1999

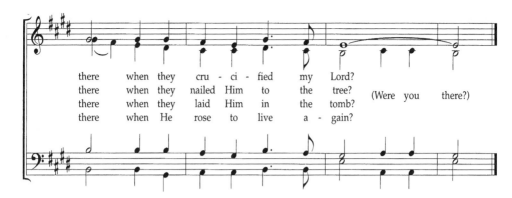

We Shall Overcome 736

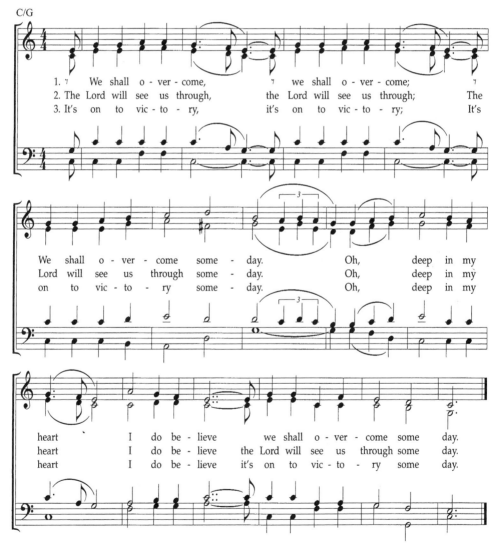

WORDS: Traditional
MUSIC: Traditional; arr. E. Sherwin Mackintosh

737 I Tried and I Tried

WORDS: Traditional
MUSIC: Traditional; arr. E. Sherwin Mackintosh

738 Would You Be Poured Out Like Wine?

WORDS: Traditional
MUSIC: Traditional; arr. E. Sherwin Mackintosh

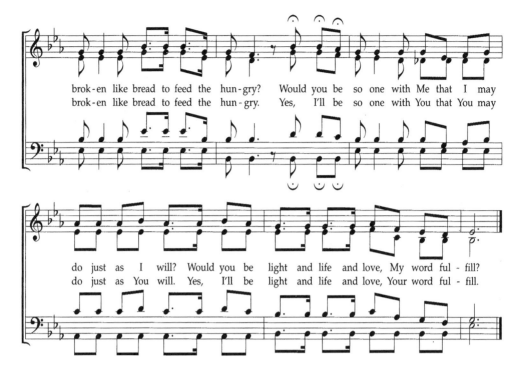

Walking on the Heaven Road 739

WORDS: Norman Starks, 1992
MUSIC: Norman Starks, 1992
© 1992 Norman Starks. All rights reserved. Used by permission.

Special Arrangements

This section of the book encompasses

- songs which would most likely be performed as a choir or as a special performance, rather than congregational singing, primarily due to the challenging natue of the music.

- rearrangements or alternative arrangements of traditional songs. In this case, the traditional or most well-known arrangement is included in the main section of the book, and the alternative arrangement can be found in this section.

800 Amazing Grace

WORDS: John Newton, 1779
MUSIC: Traditional; arr. E. Sherwin Mackintosh, 1989

Theme Song for the 1985 Boston World Missions Seminar
WORDS: Kevin Darby, 1985
MUSIC: Kevin Darby, 1985
© 1985 by Boston Church of Christ. One Merrill Street, Woburn, Mass. 01801-4629. All rights reserved. Used by permission.

803 God Alone

WORDS: Holly Jurgensen, 1997
MUSIC: Holly Jurgensen, 1997
© 1997 Discipleship Publications International. All rights reserved.

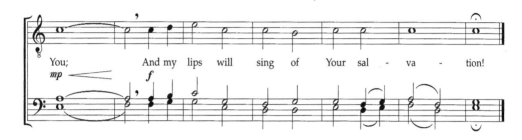

Psalm 51

For the director of music. A psalm of David. When the prophet Nathan came to him after David had committed adultery with Bathsheba.

Cleanse me with hyssop, and I will be clean;
    wash me, and I will be whiter than snow.
Let me hear joy and gladness;
    let the bones you have crushed rejoice.
Hide your face from my sins
    and blot out all my iniquity.
Create in me a pure heart, O God,
    and renew a steadfast spirit within me.
Do not cast me from your presence
    or take your Holy Spirit from me.
Restore to me the joy of your salvation
    and grant me a willing spirit, to sustain me.
Then I will teach transgressors your ways,
    and sinners will turn back to you.
Save me from bloodguilt, O God,
      the God who saves me,
    and my tongue will sing of your
        righteousness.

805 Jesus Is Lord

WORDS: Traditional (verse 2: Joseph M. Scriven, 1855)
MUSIC: Traditional; arr. Kevin Darby, 1987

Hallelujah Chorus 880

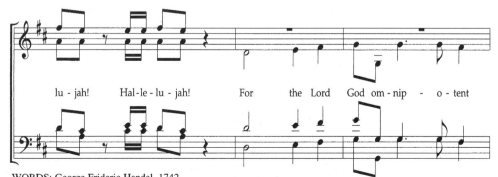

WORDS: George Frideric Handel, 1742
MUSIC: George Frideric Handel, 1742

Devotional & Children's Songs

2. Ain't no tree gonna lift its branches; I'll lift my hands to glorify His holy name.
3. Ain't no bird gonna sing in my place; I'll lift my voice to glorify His holy name.

WORDS: Lamarquis Jefferson, 1987
MUSIC: Lamarquis Jefferson, 1987
©1987 Integrity's Praise! Music / BMI c/o Integrity Music, Inc., 1000 Cody Rd., Mobile, Ala. 36695.
International copyright secured. All rights reserved. Used by permission.

901 We Are Soldiers in the Army

*Use a different name on each verse.
WORDS: Traditional
MUSIC: Traditional

Ha-La-La-La-Le-Lu-Jah 902

1. Give a big hug to the one next to you;
   Give a big hug and sing along.
   Give a big hug to the one next to you;
   Give a big hug and sing

2. Give a big smile to the one next to you;
   Give a big smile and sing along.
   Give a big smile to the one next to you;
   Give a big smile and sing

WORDS: Traditional
MUSIC: Traditional

Deep Down in My Heart 903

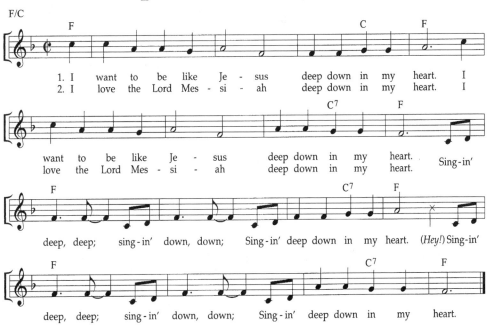

WORDS: Traditional
MUSIC: Traditional

904 Give Me Oil in My Lamp

WORDS: Traditional, A. Sevison
MUSIC: Traditional, A. Sevison

His Banner over Me Is Love 905

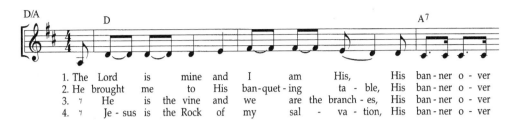
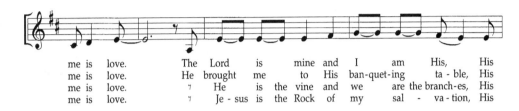

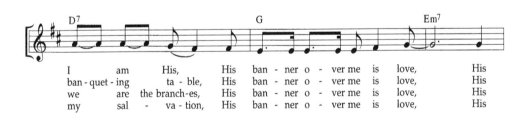
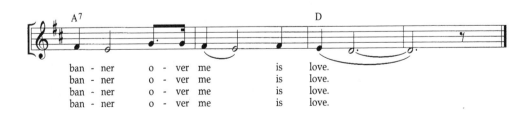

WORDS: Traditional
MUSIC: Traditional

906   I Tried and I Tried

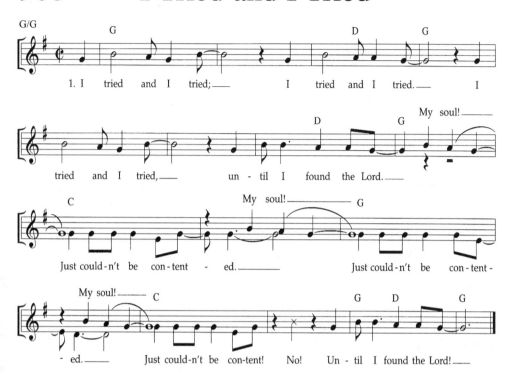

2. I searched and I searched...
3. I prayed and I prayed...
4. I cried and I cried...
5. I found, yes I found... I finally found the Lord!

WORDS: Traditional
MUSIC: Traditional

907   I'm Happy Today

2. I'm singing today...
3. I'm praying today...
4. I'm sharing today...

WORDS: Traditional
MUSIC: Traditional

This Little Light of Mine 908

2. When I'm with my parent...
3. When I'm at the playground...
4. All around my neighborhood...
5. Let it shine till Jesus comes...
6. Hide it under a bushel, NO!...
7. Won't let Satan blow it out...

WORDS: Traditional
MUSIC: Traditional

I'm Gonna View That Holy City 909

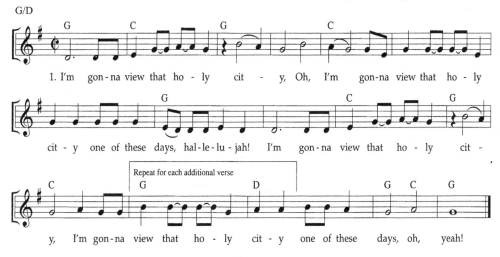

2. I'm gonna see my loving Jesus...
3. I'm gonna sit at the welcome table...
4. I'm gonna feast on milk and honey...
5. I'm gonna sing and never get tired...
6. I'm gonna make my home in heaven...
7. I'm gonna meet with Paul and Peter...
8. I'm gonna praise my precious Savior...

WORDS: Traditional
MUSIC: Traditional

910 Jesus Loves the Little Children

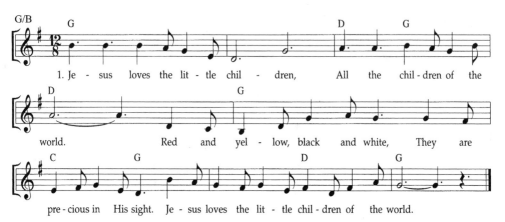

2. Jesus died for all the children...
3. Jesus rose for all the children...
4. Jesus lives for all the children...

WORDS: Traditional
MUSIC: Traditional

911 In My Father's House

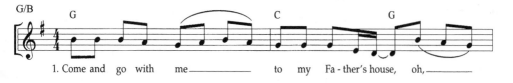

2. There are many rooms...
3. We're gonna have a good time...
4. Everything's all right...

WORDS: Traditional
MUSIC: Traditional

I've Got the Joy, Joy, Joy   912

2. I've got the peace that passes understanding...
3. I've got the love of Jesus...
4. I've got the wonderful love of my blessed redeemer way down in depths of my heart.

WORDS: Traditional
MUSIC: Traditional

Love, Love, Love   913

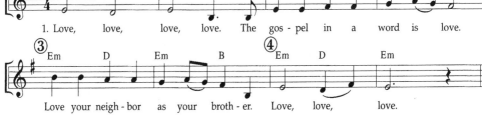

2. Peace, peace, peace, peace. The gospel in a word is peace.
   Peace that passes understanding. Peace, peace, peace.

3. Joy, joy, joy, joy. The gospel in a word is joy.
   Joy that fills to overflowing. Joy, joy, joy.

4. Christ, Christ, Christ, Christ. The gospel in a word is Christ.
   Love him, serve him and adore him. Christ, Christ, Christ.

WORDS: Traditional
MUSIC: Traditional

914 The Christian Jubilee

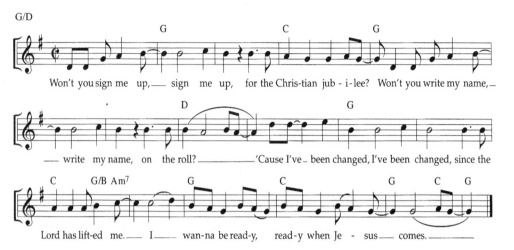

WORDS: Traditional
MUSIC: Traditional

915 Oh, Be Careful

2. Oh, be careful, little ears, what you hear...
3. Oh, be careful, little mouth, what you say...
4. Oh, be careful, little hands, what you touch...

WORDS: Traditional
MUSIC: Traditional

My God Is So Great 916

My God is so great, so strong and so might-y, there's noth-ing my God can-not do! *clap! clap!* My

God is so great, so strong and so might-y, there's noth-ing my God can-not do! *clap! clap!* The

moun-tains are His, the riv-ers are His, the stars are His hand-i-work too. My

God is so great, so strong and so might-y, there's noth-ing my God can-not do! *clap! clap!*

WORDS: Traditional
MUSIC: Traditional

Roll the Gospel Chariot 917

You've got to roll the gos-pel char-i-ot a-long. Come on and

roll the gos-pel char-i-ot a-long. You've got to roll the gos-pel

char-i-ot a-long. And we won't tag a-long be-hind.

1. If my brother's in the way, we will stop and pick him up.
2. If my sister's in the way, we will stop and pick her up.
3. If the devil's in the way, we will roll right over him.

WORDS: Traditional
MUSIC: Traditional

918 Rejoice in the Lord Always

WORDS: Traditional
MUSIC: Traditional

919 Praise Him, Praise Him

2. Love Him, love Him, all ye little children...
3. Thank Him, thank Him, all ye little children...
4. Serve Him, serve Him, all ye little children...

WORDS: Traditional
MUSIC: Traditional

Peace Like a River 920

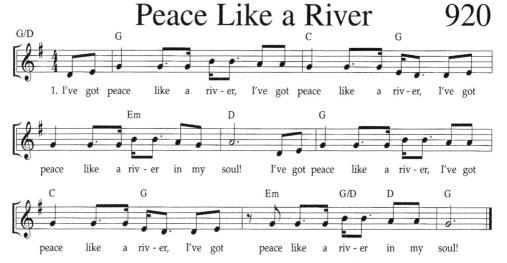

2. I've got love like an ocean...
3. I've got joy like a fountain...
4. I've got peace like a river, I've got love like an ocean, I've got joy like a fountain in my soul...

WORDS: Traditional
MUSIC: Traditional

Whose Side Are You Fightin' On? 921

For additional verses use "singin' on," "prayin' on," "lovin' on," "servin' on" etc.
WORDS: Traditional
MUSIC: Traditional

922 Rise and Shine

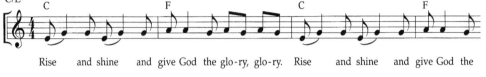

1. The Lord said to Noah
   There's gonna be a floody, floody.
   Lord said to Noah
   There's gonna be a floody, floody.
   Get those children out of the muddy, muddy,
   Children of the Lord.

2. The Lord told Noah
   To build him an arky, arky.
   Lord told Noah
   To build him an arky, arky.
   Build it out of gopher barky, barky,
   Children of the Lord.

3. The animals they came in
   They came in by twosies, twosies.
   Animals they came in
   They came in by twosies, twosies.
   Elephants and kangaroosies, roosies,
   Children of the Lord.

4. It rained and it poured
   For forty nights and daysies, daysies.
   Rained and it poured
   For forty nights and daysies, daysies.
   Nearly drove those animals crazies, crazies,
   Children of the Lord.

5. The sun came out and
   Dried up the landy, landy.
   The sun came out and
   Dried up all the landy, landy.
   Everything was fine and dandy, dandy,
   Children of the Lord.

6. That is the end of,
   The end of my story, story.
   That is the end of,
   The end of my story, story.
   Everything is hunky dory, dory,
   Children of the Lord.

WORDS: Traditional
MUSIC: Traditional

Standin' in the Need of Prayer   923

It's me, it's me, it's me, O Lord,   Stand-in' in the need of prayer.
It's me,

1. Not my fa-ther or my moth-er;
2. Not my broth-er or my sis-ter; But, it's me, O Lord,   Stand-in' in the need of   prayer.
3. Not the eld-ers or the dea-cons;

Not my fa-ther or my moth-er;
Not my broth-er or my sis-ter; But, it's me, O Lord,   Stand-in' in the need of   prayer.
Not the eld-ers or the dea-cons;

WORDS: Traditional spiritual
MUSIC: Traditional spiritual

Psalm 142:1, 5-7

A maskil of David. When he was in the cave. A prayer.

I cry aloud to the Lord;
    I lift up my voice to the Lord for mercy.
…I cry to you, O Lord;
    I say: "You are my refuge,
        my portion in the land of the living."
Listen to my cry,
    for I am in desperate need;
rescue me from those who pursue me,
    for they are too strong for me.
Set me free from my prison,
    that I may praise your name.
Then the righteous will gather about me
    because of your goodness to me.

924 The New Testament Song

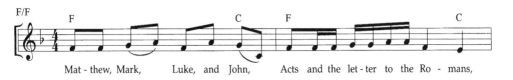
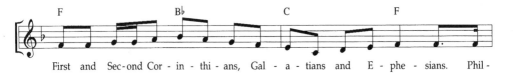
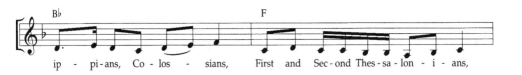

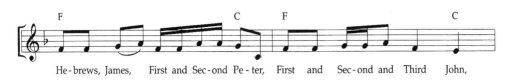

WORDS: Traditional
MUSIC: Traditional

Show Me the Way 925

2. The woman sat by the well and she cried...show me the way...
3. Jesus hung on the cross and He died...I am the way...
4. Jesus rose from the dead and He cried...show them the way...

WORDS: Traditional
MUSIC: Traditional

The Sea of Galilee 926

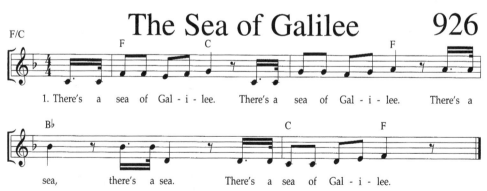

2. There's a boat in the sea of Galilee...
3. There are men in the boat on the sea of Galilee...
4. There are hands on the men in the boat on the sea of Galilee...
5. There are nets in the hands of the men in the boat on the sea of Galilee...
6. There are fish in the nets in the hands of the men in the boat on the sea of Galilee...
7. There are many, many fish in the nets in the hands of the men in the boat on the Sea of Galilee!

WORDS: Traditional
MUSIC: Traditional

927 This Is the Day

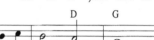

2. Jesus is the way, Jesus is the way that the Lord has made...
3. This is the day, this is the day when he rose again...
4. This is the day, this is the day when the Spirit came...

WORDS: Traditional
MUSIC: Traditional

928 This Is My Commandment

WORDS: Traditional
MUSIC: Traditional

The Wise Man 929

1. The wise man built his house up-on the rock. The
2. The fool-ish man built his house up-on the sand. The
3. So build your house on the Lord Je-sus Christ. So

wise man built his house up-on the rock. The wise man built his
fool-ish man built his house up-on the sand. The fool-ish man built his
build your house on the Lord Je-sus Christ. So build your house on the

house up-on the rock, And the rains came tum-bling down. Oh!
house up-on the sand; And the rains came tum-bling down. Oh!
Lord Je-sus Christ; And the bless-ings come tum-bling down. Oh!

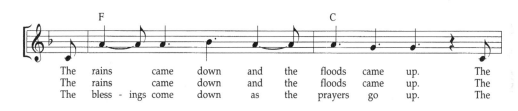
The rains came down and the floods came up. The
The rains came down and the floods came up. The
The bless-ings come down as the prayers go up. The

rains came down and the floods came up. The rains came down and the
rains came down and the floods came up. The rains came down and the
bless-ings come down as the prayers go up. The bless-ings come down as the

floods came up; And the wise man's house stood firm. But!
floods came up; And the fool-ish man's house went splat! So!
prayers go up; So build your house on the Lord.

WORDS: Traditional
MUSIC: Traditional

930 King of the Jungle

WORDS: Traditional
MUSIC: Traditional

Show Me the Way 925

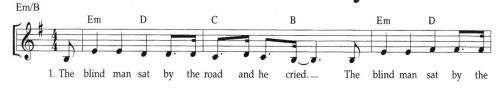

2. The woman sat by the well and she cried...show me the way...
3. Jesus hung on the cross and He died...I am the way...
4. Jesus rose from the dead and He cried...show them the way...

WORDS: Traditional
MUSIC: Traditional

The Sea of Galilee 926

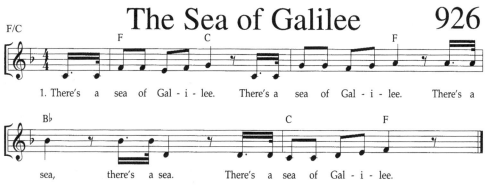

2. There's a boat in the sea of Galilee...
3. There are men in the boat on the sea of Galilee...
4. There are hands on the men in the boat on the sea of Galilee...
5. There are nets in the hands of the men in the boat on the sea of Galilee...
6. There are fish in the nets in the hands of the men in the boat on the sea of Galilee...
7. There are many, many fish in the nets in the hands of the men in the boat on the Sea of Galilee!

WORDS: Traditional
MUSIC: Traditional

927 This Is the Day

1. This is the day, this is the day that the Lord has made, that the Lord has made. We will re-joice, we will re-joice and be glad in it, and be glad in it. Oh, this is the day that the Lord has made. Let us re-joice and be glad in it. This is the day, this is the day that the Lord has made.

2. Jesus is the way, Jesus is the way that the Lord has made...
3. This is the day, this is the day when he rose again...
4. This is the day, this is the day when the Spirit came...

WORDS: Traditional
MUSIC: Traditional

928 This Is My Commandment

This is my com-mand-ment that you love one an-oth-er, that your joy may be full.
This is my com-mand-ment that you love one an-oth-er, that your joy may be full.
That your joy may be full, that your joy may be full.
This is my com-mand-ment that you love one an-oth-er, that your joy may be full.

WORDS: Traditional
MUSIC: Traditional

The Wise Man 929

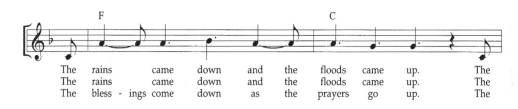

WORDS: Traditional
MUSIC: Traditional

930 King of the Jungle

1. Who's the king of the jungle? Ooh! Ooh! Who's the king of the sea? Bubble bubble bubble. Who's the king of the universe? And who's the king of me? His name is J-E-S-U-S Yes! He's the king of me. He's the king of the universe, the jungle and the sea, Bubble, bubble, bubble.

2. Who's the king of the desert? Blah, blah! Who's the king of the stars? Twinkle, twinkle, twinkle. Who's the king of the Milky Way? And who's the king of Mars? His name is J-E-S-U-S Yes! He's the king of me, He's the king of the Milky Way, the desert and the stars Twinkle, twinkle, twinkle.

Ending: You know it's J-E-S-U-S, Yes! He's the king of me. It's J-E-S-U-S, Yes!

WORDS: Traditional
MUSIC: Traditional

I'm in the Lord's Army 931

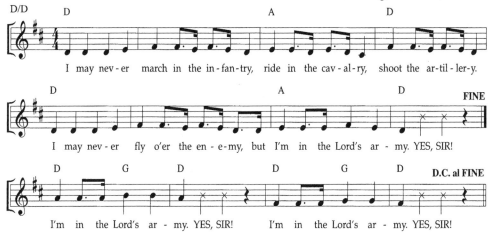

WORDS: Traditional
MUSIC: Traditional

Building Up the Kingdom 932

WORDS: Traditional
MUSIC: Traditional

933 Jesus Is Well and Alive Today

WORDS: Gary L. Mabry, 1971
MUSIC: Gary L. Mabry, 1971
© 1971 Boston Music Co., 116 Boylston St., Boston, Mass. 02116. This arrangement © 1974 Boston Music Company. International copyright secured. Made in U.S.A. All rights reserved. Used by permission.

Romans 8:37-39

No, in all these things we are more than conquerors through him who loved us. For I am convinced that neither death nor life, neither angels nor demons, neither the present nor the future, nor any powers, neither height nor depth, nor anything else in all creation, will be able to separate us from the love of God that is in Christ Jesus our Lord.